The Comprehensive

Education Policy Perspectives

General Editor: Professor Ivor Goodson, Faculty of Education,
University of Western Ontario, London,
Canada N6G 1G7

Education policy analysis has long been a neglected area in the United Kingdom and, to an extent, in the USA and Australia. The result has been a profound gap between the study of education and the formulation of education policy. For practitioners such a lack of analysis of the new policy initiatives has worrying implications particularly at such a time of policy flux and change. Education policy has, in recent years, been a matter for intense political debate — the political and public interest in the working of the system has come at the same time as the consensus on education policy has been broken by the advent of the 'New Right'. As never before the political parties and pressure groups differ in their articulated policies and prescriptions for the education sector. Critical thinking about these developments is clearly necessary.

All those working within the system also need information on policy making, policy implementation and effective day-to-day operation. Pressure on schools from government, education authorities and parents has generated an enormous need for knowledge amongst those on the receiving end of educational policies.

This series aims to fill the academic gap, to reflect the politicalization of education, and to provide the practitioners with the analysis for informed implementation of policies that they will need. It will offer studies in broad areas of policy studies. Beside the general section it will offer a particular focus in the following areas: School organization and improvement (David Reynolds, University College, Cardiff, UK); Critical social analysis (Professor Philip Wexler, University of Rochester, USA); Policy studies and evaluation (Professor Ernest House, University of Colorado-Boulder, USA); and Education and training (Dr Peter Cuttance, University of Edinburgh, UK).

School Organization and Improvement Series
Editor: David Reynolds, University College, Cardiff, UK

Education Policy Perspectives

The Comprehensive Experiment

A Comparison of the Selective and Non-selective Systems of School Organization

David Reynolds and
Michael Sullivan
with Stephen Murgatroyd

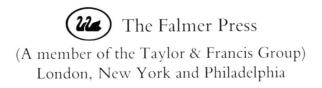 The Falmer Press

(A member of the Taylor & Francis Group)
London, New York and Philadelphia

UK   The Falmer Press, Falmer House, Barcombe, Lewes, East Sussex, BN8 5DL

USA   The Falmer Press, Taylor & Francis Inc., 242 Cherry Street, Philadelphia, PA 19106-1906

First published 1987

Library of Congress Cataloguing in Publication Data is available on request

ISBN 1-85000-210-X
ISBN 1-85000-211-8 (pbk.)

Jacket design by Caroline Archer

Typeset in 10/12 Bembo by
Imago Publishing Ltd, Thame, Oxon

Printed in Great Britain by Taylor & Francis (Printers) Ltd, Basingstoke

Contents

The comprehensive school is in danger of
becoming something everybody knows about but
which very few understand

ILEA Education Booklet

Acknowledgements

This is the third in a series of eight studies that have taken us over a decade to research and write. As before, our major debt is to the headteachers, teachers, pupils and parents who have given us the benefit of their experience as providers and consumers of education. The continued agreement of the headteachers, schools and the local education authority responsible for education in 'Treliw', our anonymous community, to allow us virtually unrestricted access to their schools is also something that we are very grateful for. The work reported here was made possible by a grant from the Education Department of the Welsh Office to University College, Cardiff and we are grateful to Welsh Office staff for their encouragement, advice and forbearance in the face of our consistent inability to keep to deadlines. Mistakes, errors, omissions and misinterpretations we, as all authors, claim as our own.

David Reynolds
Michael Sullivan
Stephen Murgatroyd
Autumn 1986

Introduction

Comprehensive schools have been in existence in Britain for over forty years. At present they educate over 80 per cent of British children attending state secondary schools. In many countries, schools like these are the normal form of secondary education.

Controversy about comprehensive schools and their supposed failures has been a dominant feature of the last decade. Many have seen them as not maintaining the academic standards of the grammar school. There have been attempts to link the increasing manifestations of youthful disorder like football hooliganism with the schools' supposed failure to socially control their less able pupils. From defenders of the schools have come reminders of the poor standards of education of the past selective system and the belief that the schools, if adequately resourced, can begin over time to develop the academic and social talents of young people more than the parts of the old selective system.

Protagonists and commentators have much to say about the schools but unfortunately the battle is based upon emotion and personal commitment, not upon evidence. Surprisingly little research has been done on the comprehensive school, especially since its introduction was perhaps the major educational change since 1870. Surprisingly little research has compared the comprehensive and the selective systems and that which has done this has invariably looked at comprehensive schools creamed of their high ability pupils.

This book reports the result of a unique experiment in order to shed some scientific evidence on the debate about the schools. A community in Wales wanted to change its educational system in the mid-1970s — half the community went comprehensive but the other half, because the buildings available were unsuitable, stayed selective. Both systems ran in parallel for four years and we studied the children that they received, the way the systems were run and the successes and failures that they recorded with their children. The data on the pupils is provided in two ways — from a sample of 11-year-old boys who were being studied as part of a delinquency project, and from a much larger sample of both sexes and all ages. The data on the schools was gathered by us as part of our ten-year research programme in our anonymous community of Treliw.

The book is in three sections. Part 1 looks at the national comprehensive experiment and chapter 1 outlines the history of comprehensive school development over the last 100 years, together with explaining the precise reasons why comprehensive education became a Labour policy thirty years ago. Chapter 2 looks at the research evidence on the schools and asks the question — have the schools nationally attained the goals that have been outlined for them?

Part 2 looks in detail at our local comprehensive experiment Chapter 3 outlines our research community, its history and its past and present educational system, together with our research strategy and design. The relative effectiveness of the two different systems on their children's academic and social development is outlined in chapter 4 and the processes within the two systems that can account for the major differences between them are the subject of chapter 5.

Part 3 and chapter 6 summarizes our findings and outlines our recommendations as to what the implications of our work are for the organization and management of comprehensive schools, and for the political and academic debate about the schools that we start the book with.

Part One: The National Picture

Chapter 1

Comprehensive Schooling — A Historical Account and an Explanation

> ... a gigantic experiment with the lives of millions of children.
>
> (Julienne Ford)

The history of educational provision in England and Wales this century is a history of change and development and nowhere is this process of change more obvious than in the provision of secondary education. In the years before 1944 only a small minority of children attended secondary schools, which levied fees for the majority of available places. For the rest, basic instruction in reading, writing and arithmetic was provided in elementary schools of one type or another. Despite the establishment of further education institutions sponsored by the labour movement, entry into the universities and the professions remained largely the privilege of a social and intellectual elite.

The 1944 Education Act effected a significant change. Under its provisions local education authorities were made responsible for providing free and compulsory secondary education for all children between the ages of 11 and 15. The majority of LEAs made such provision available in a tripartite system — an organizational pattern which remained undisturbed until the publication of Circular 10/65 by the new Labour government in July 1965. This Circular sanctioned a further significant change in secondary education by requesting LEAs to submit plans for the reorganization of secondary education along comprehensive lines. In the years following this famous Circular, the comprehensive system has gradually achieved primacy and the development of the comprehensive system of secondary education has been consistent, despite the presence from 1970 to 1974 and since May 1979 of Conservative governments somewhat hostile to the comprehensive school. Presently the system has been almost universally adopted by LEAs in England and Wales.

Although the earliest established comprehensive schools are barely thirty years old, calls for a unified secondary system of education have a much longer history. As early as 1854 Richard Cobden, the Anti Corn Law leader, was calling for a common secondary school system for all (see Rubenstein and Simon, 1973, p. 4). During the first three decades of the twentieth century a movement for common secondary schooling for all children developed. That movement united teachers' organizations, the trade union movement and others in promoting at first multilateral schools and then comprehensive schools with a common curriculum (see Parkinson, 1970; Rubenstein and Simon, 1973).

Despite the campaigns mounted by this coalition of forces, government commissions (the Spens Committee in 1938 and the Norwood Committee in 1943) reported in favour of the introduction of a segregated secondary education system (see Parkinson, 1970; Rubenstein and Simon, 1973)

The 1944 Education Act and the Labour Government

It was against such a background that the 1944 Education Bill was drafted and introduced into the House of Commons by RA Butler on behalf of the National Government. The Bill was introduced on 16 December 1943 and received the Royal Assent on 4 August 1944. During the Bill's passage there was much debate and the final Act contained implicit encouragement rather than explicit instructions that the organization of secondary education should be along segregated lines. The relevant clause of the Act (Section 8) ran:

> The schools available for an area shall not be deemed sufficient unless they are sufficient in number, character and equipment to afford for all pupils opportunities for education offering such variety of instruction and training as may be desirable in view of their different ages, abilities and aptitudes, and of the different periods for which they may be expected to remain at school.

The very fact that the clause had been drafted in this way did, of course, mean that there was no legal inhibition on the development of multilateral (or comprehensive) schools. The inhibitions — which were to prove effective buttresses against LEAs wishing to set up comprehensive schools — were to be administrative.

In 1945 a Labour government was returned. However, pledges made at earlier Labour conferences to develop a multilateral system of education were not to be honoured. On the eve of the government taking office the 'caretaker' Conservative government had published a policy statement on education, entitled *The Nation's Schools* (1945). This document argued that there already existed in embryonic form a de facto tripartite secondary education system following the Hadow reorganization (see Rubenstein and Simon, 1973) and it further argued that this system should be developed. In addition, the authors did not foresee any need to increase the number of grammar schools; this latter suggestion certainly appeared to contravene the principle said to be behind the 1944 Act that working class children should have the same opportunity to attend grammar schools as middle class children, since such a principle would have needed the provision of a greater number of grammar school places. The Conservative document claimed, on the contrary, that since in 1938 40 per cent of secondary school leavers had not taken the school certificate and 25 per cent had left before the age of 16, many children had obviously been receiving an education beyond their capabilities. In fact, the statement argued the numbers of places available in grammar school might actually be reduced. Moreover, should a larger number of working class children than before gain access to grammar school, this might mean a corresponding decrease in the number of 'talented' working class children entering industrial occupations, a situation which the Conservatives believed would damage the economy by creating a smaller pool of skilled labour.

Despite the fact that this policy statement ran counter to the policy of the Labour party at conference, it was to be accepted as the basis of government policy by the first Labour Minister of Education — Ellen Wilkinson. Within the post-war Labour party there was to be a constant battle between the two Labour ministers of this period and pressure groups for comprehensive education.

The Minister firmly defended tripartism, claiming that parity in material resources between different types of schools would lead to parity of esteem. In addition, she argued that distinctions between the schools were made on the basis of objective educational criteria and not, as had previously been the case, on the basis of unjustifiable social criteria. When Wilkinson died in 1947 her successor published almost immediately a policy statement *The New Secondary Education*. Though this document had been prepared during the tenure of the previous Minister he defined its defence of tripartitism as his own.

A Movement Away from Multilateralism and the First Comprehensive Schools

In the years following the end of the war there was a discernible movement by teacher organizations away from the concept of multilateralism. Those organizations which had helped pioneer the multilateral idea in the twenties and thirties noticeably cooled in their enthusiasm following the passage of the 1944 Act. This movement was particularly obvious among grammar school teachers who perhaps felt that the promised equality of status for other types of secondary school could lower their own status, a view given expression in an article by Eric James, High Master of Manchester Grammar School, who argued that the common school would inevitably produce 'grave social, educational and cultural evils' and 'may well be a national disaster' (James, 1947). The same author claimed, in a book published two years later, that such schools would lead to 'a narrowing and impoverishment of the whole content of education' (James, 1949). Various commentators, among them HC Dent (1970), claimed educational segregation to be an English tradition. Of perhaps greater significance is the fact that the NUT conference in 1948 heavily defeated a motion opposing tripartism.

It is paradoxical that in this politically inauspicious period the first comprehensive schools were established and ironic that some of the pioneering authorities were controlled by Conservative councils, when the Conservative party at a national level opposed comprehensivization. Immediately LEAs had been asked to produce development plans for a secondary education system in their areas, some had set about producing plans for comprehensive education. The London School Plan, adopted by the London County Council in 1947, envisaged the establishment of 103 comprehensive schools. Coventry, which had been extensively bomb-damaged during the war, planned for comprehensive schools to cater for 80 per cent of its pupils. The rural areas of Westmoreland, Anglesey and the Isle of Man planned a similar reorganization, as did the county boroughs of Southend, Oldham, Bradford, Bolton and the counties of the West Riding and Middlesex (see Saran, 1973, for an account of the latter).

The plans for reorganization in Middlesex were quickly rejected by the Ministry, which allowed only a limited experiment with the establishment of two 'comprehensive' schools. The London Plan was similarly rejected, as was the plan by the West Riding. The development of new types of secondary school did occur, however, in Anglesey and in the Isle of Man (which was not in any case subject to British Parliamentary controls). Indeed, in areas of scattered population comprehensive schooling was accepted by both major political parties as a desirable solution. The LCC was allowed five experimental 'interim' comprehensive schools by merging selective central schools with modern schools but was prevented from absorbing any grammar schools into comprehensive schools. The development, then, was severely limited by the Ministry during this period but the seeds of comprehensive education were being sown.

Political and Educational Polarization: The Movement Develops

The general election of 1951 sent the Labour Party into opposition, a position it was to occupy for thirteen years. During these years the parliamentary party was to move gradually and painfully to the acceptance of some sort of comprehensive education policy as party policy for secondary education. This move was accompanied by (and perhaps itself provoked) a move towards complete opposition to comprehensivization by the Conservative party. This period also saw the production of sociological and psychological evidence questioning the accuracy of selection procedures for secondary education and questioning the whole basis of selection itself. This evidence was to be used to support the claims of the comprehensive school advocates both inside and outside of the Labour Party and was supported by other evidence on the wastage of talent in the selective system. Conservative governments of this period, however, remained in large part hostile to further reorganization.

The comprehensive school issue was kept alive during these years by the interplay of four factors; the continuing debate in the Labour party, the attitude to comprehensive schooling in the Conservative party, the publication of sociological and psychological evidence about the tripartite system; and changes in the attitudes of parents towards it.

The Labour Debate

Firstly, as usually seems to be the case, the Labour Party was a more unified force in opposition than they had been in government. The trend set by the growing number of MPs who supported the comprehensive idea in the last years of government was confirmed by the publication of the document *A Policy for Secondary Education* (1951) which sought to commit the Labour party to a policy of total comprehensive reorganization. This commitment was reinforced by a statement in favour of comprehensivization at the 1952 conference by the NEC spokesman, Alice Bacon, who nevertheless warned conference that the chances of such a reorganization were diminishing as the tripartite system became further established. She urged LEAs controlled by Labour to take more notice of conference decisions, remarking that many had accepted the tripartite system because they saw it as having been encouraged by a Labour government. The NEC, anxious to generate momentum on the issue, set up a Social Services Sub-committee to review the structure of education which reported in 1953.

The conclusions of the Sub-committee, substantially accepted by the NEC, were published in a document entitled *Challenge to Britain* (1953). The section on comprehensive secondary education attacked the 11+ selection procedure because it labelled children at an early age as belonging to different educational 'types' and segregated them, a segregation which was usually permanent as transfers from secondary modern schools to grammar schools were usually hindered by curriculum differences. By contrast, the comprehensive school was portrayed in the report as delaying, rather than eliminating, selection and as offering all children education in one school in the studies to which they were most suited. Any early judgments concerning the child's ability and aptitude would, the argument ran, be subject to regular review in the comprehensive school — arrangements being sufficiently flexible that they could easily be altered. The report went on to suggest that comprehensive education might be implemented in a variety of equally acceptable ways, including the all-through (11–18) comprehensive school or (as in Leicestershire) by means of junior comprehensive schools offering an undifferential curriculum to all pupils aged 11–15 but with some pupils (whose parents wished) transferring at age 15 to a senior comprehensive school.

The document came under heavy attack even before it reached Labour party conference. Delegates at the National Association of Labour Teachers in 1953 argued that the variety of plans suggested in the document was unsatisfactory: the establishment of split junior and senior comprehensive schools could lessen the number of working class children staying on at school since parental, social and economic pressures might prevent many from making the transfer from junior to senior school at 15. In turn this would reduce the opportunities of such children to compete for higher paid occupations by removing the GCE examination from their reach. Further, delegates suggested that the split school would sharpen rather than blunt social distinctions because the gulf between ordinary school leavers and those who transferred to senior school would be wider than that which currently existed between the grammar school and modern school leavers. Finally they stated such a system would serve to make the raising of the school leaving age to 16 harder to achieve as it would effect a natural administrative break at age 15. The annual Labour party conference reached substantially the same conclusions, as a result of which a number of delegates offered to redraft the document to conform to the demands of the NALT amendment calling for 'all through' 11–18 schools. The statement reappeared later in the year retaining the split school idea in a relegated position but making a clear commitment to the principle of the all through (11–18) school.

Hard on the heels of the firm commitment to comprehensive education made by Labour party conferences in 1952 and 1953 followed a concern about how to present the policy to the electorate and how to implement the policy when the Labour party was returned to government. Margaret Cole, in a memorandum, suggested the need for ensuring party unity on the issue before presenting Labour's plans to the electorate. Such internal unity was necessary, she argued, to persuade reluctant LEAs to implement a comprehensive policy when the Labour party returned to power because 'it is no part of Labour's intention to force LEAs to embark on new experiments'. In expressing this view she opened a debate within the party about the use of legislation in introducing the comprehensive policy which was to continue over the next two decades. NALT and the Publicity and Policy Sub-Committee demurred from the point of view expressed in the memorandum, claiming that if the policy was to be implemented successfully Labour would have to introduce legislation compelling comprehensivization.

Labour attitudes to comprehensivization were further influenced by the results of a poll in 1957 which showed widespread ignorance of the issue of comprehensive education among the public and little opposition to segregation, together with great respect for the grammar school.

These findings affected the views of the Labour Party concerning the type of propaganda which should be used in a campaign in favour of comprehensive education and the study group working on this question supported the idea that the appeal of the comprehensive school probably lay in emphasizing the educational benefit which could be derived from it by children who would have failed to go to grammar school. Simply, this group came to the conclusion that the comprehensive school should be presented as 'a grammar school for all' if the policy were to be electorally attractive.

Perhaps as a result of this and other factors the parliamentary leadership appeared to be in retreat from a strong definition of comprehensive education and in the run-up to the 1959 election not all of the leadership were convinced that the orthodox, all-through school was the answer to the problems of secondary education. In fact, Hugh Gaitskell, the Labour leader, seemed to lead this retreat from a strong comprehensive policy.

In a public speech in 1958 he argued that the term 'comprehensive' did not mean that all children should attend the same kind of huge impersonal school — instead, it meant 'something simpler than that, that we abandon the idea of permanent segregation'. This speech cast an aura of uncertainty around what Labour's policy would be on return to government. The core of Gaitskell's argument was the abolition of permanent selection. Beyond this many arrangements seemed permissible.

In 1959 Roy Jenkins, in his book *The Labour Case*, argued for the retention of the 'good, established grammar school' to act as a bridge between the state sector and the private sector. In his scheme comprehensive schools would play only a limited role, being created where new schools were built or where reorganization was necessary for other reasons. Such a view was supported by Manny Shinwell who criticized the Labour party for sacrificing the grammar school which gave many working class children an opportunity for advancement, while it feared to intervene more widely in secondary education by opposing the continued existence of the public school sector.

This retreat by leading members of the party threw the party into disarray. However, *Learning to Live* — published in 1958 — showed that the leadership view had gained ascendancy in the struggle over the form of comprehensive education. Whilst the document repeated Labour's commitment to comprehensive education, it included an explicit commitment *against* the use of legislation to reorganize secondary education and although it remained ambivalent on the question of the future of the comprehensive school, it seemed to be presenting it as an institution which would replicate the important features and traditions of the grammar school and would be, in Gaitskell's phrase, 'a grammar school for all'. It was this sort of conception of comprehensive education, allied with an emphasis on the wastage of talent in the tripartite system, that Harold Wilson, the new leader of the Labour party, was to advocate in his famous 'science and socialism' speech to the 1963 party conference.

The Attitude of the Conservative Party

During its thirteen years in government between 1951 and 1964 the Conservative party moved to a position of hostility to the idea of the comprehensive school. In the early years the Ministry was prepared to sanction certain limited experiments with comprehensive schools but only if the LEAs concerned were to initiate the reorganization. Such experiments were only sanctioned, however, if they took place within the context of a set of selective schools. Any proposals to merge a grammar school with other schools to form a comprehensive school were rejected, a policy which continued when the first Conservative Minister, Florence Horsborough, was succeeded by Sir David Eccles. His view was that it was impossible to enlarge the nation's 'grammar' school stream without changing the character of higher education and the grammar school. The solution to the increased demand and need for a higher standard of secondary education was to be found, he believed, in the improvement of the secondary modern schools and not in the reorganization of the secondary school system. Though Eccles was succeeded in 1962 by Edward Boyle, who was less hostile to the idea of the comprehensive school, attitudes within the Conservative party had hardened to such an extent that he seemed powerless to act against the views of the majority of the Conservative party against the comprehensive school.

Paradoxically, while the two major parties' positions on comprehensive education became increasingly polarized in Parliament, developments were taking place in some LEAs which were completely different to the positions taken by the national parties. Many Labour controlled LEAs were reluctant even to seek permission to establish comprehensive schools and some Conservative authorities, like Leicestershire, were in the vanguard of the development of the small number of such schools opened in this period.

Though the political battle continued to rage in the decade and a half before the publication of Circular 10/65, these years also saw the generation of a great deal of evidence from government reports and independent research studies that the process of selection which lay at the core of the tripartite system was functioning both to produce a wastage of talent and to create inequality of educational opportunity. The impact of this research was marked (see Reynolds and Sullivan, 1980).

Evidence from Sociological and Psychological Research Studies

The work of Halsey and Gardner (1953) and Floud (1957) demonstrated that children of manual workers who possessed grammar school ability according to the criteria then used were under-represented in grammar schools and that the children of middle class parents were over-represented. The National Foundation for Educational Research (NFER) claimed also that even the best available tests which sought to measure ability at 11 had a 10 per cent margin of error in the selection of children to one or other type of secondary school. The Crowther Report (1959) published results of a survey carried out among recruits to the armed services, which showed that a substantial number of the sons of manual workers in their sample had been wrongly placed at the secondary school stage. All these findings suggested that the intelligence tests used to sort out the academic sheep from the non-academic goats were massively unequal to the task.

Moreover, further evidence was becoming available at this time, which questioned the whole theory on which the intelligence test rested. Vernon (1957) questioned the extent to which intelligence as measured in the intelligence test was an inherited characteristic and Bernstein (1959) suggested that the poor academic performance of working class children might merely reflect a lack of knowledge of the formal language used in educational settings but not used in the public language of their homes. Douglas (1964) also presented a framework to understand how an interlocking network of inequalities operated to the detriment of working class children in terms of depressing their educational achievement. Further evidence on the wastage of high ability, mostly working class, children was provided by Crowther and numerous other studies.

The rationale and operation of the tripartite system was thrown into question by these and other findings. In effect, as Halsey noted, a rapidly expanding technical economy was being ill-served by a system of secondary education which functioned to confirm initial social status (since privileged middle class children were associated with the grammar school) rather than making status dependent upon merit. Wastage of ability — particularly of working class children — was economically unsound and morally indefensible in the view of Halsey and other Fabians (see Reynolds and Sullivan, 1980).

Changes in the Schools and Changing Attitudes Among Parents

The ground upon which the tripartite system stood was further shaken during the late 1950s by the changes taking place within the tripartite system itself and by the changing attitudes of a vocal section of the population to the operation of the system.

One of the fundamental arguments used by earlier supporters of the tripartite system was that only *some* children were capable of the abstract conceptualization necessary in an academic education, whilst others did not possess such capabilities. However, in the late fifties changes occurred in the curriculum and examination policy of grammar and secondary modern schools which made a nonsense of this already discredited distinction. Firstly, as the children of the post-war 'baby boom' achieved secondary school age a smaller proportion of the 11-year-old population gained grammar school places (as no extra provision had been made), which resulted in secondary modern schools receiving children from a much wider section of the ability range than before. Many secondary modern schools responded to this change by developing a more academic curriculum for some of their pupils, entering growing numbers of pupils for GCE 'O' level examinations and developing sixth-forms. The conceptual framework of the tripartite system was challenged, as it was also by a broadening of the curriculum to allow more vocational subjects to be taught in the grammar schools. Grammar and secondary modern schools came to resemble each other more.

Running parallel to these changes and resulting from the broader social class composition of the modern schools, there evolved pressure from largely middle class parents against the selective system. This pressure reflected the failure of considerable numbers of middle class children to get to the grammar school, a hitherto unknown phenomenon.

To summarize, the time of Tory government from 1951 to 1964 saw a movement in the Labour opposition towards full acceptance of the need for comprehensive reorganisation, though the concept of the goals of the comprehensive school appears to have undergone substantial redefinition by the parliamentary leadership. At the same time the Conservative party had sanctioned the establishment of comprehensive schools in extraordinary circumstances only and appeared to have moved by the early sixties to a position of overt hostility to the comprehensive school idea, seeing it as the product of socialist 'egalitarian' ideology. Dissatisfaction with selection in secondary education had been aided in the late fifties, however, by the publication of research findings which questioned the accuracy of the predictive intelligence test and also the notion of inherited general intelligence, together with findings that showed inequality of opportunity between classes and a wastage of talent from certain social classes.

The Labour Government and Circular 10/65

In October 1964 a Labour government was elected and Michael Stewart became Minister of Education. In January 1965 he declared his intention to issue a Circular to initiate comprehensive reorganization of the secondary education sector. In fact he was replaced as Minister by Anthony Crosland in April 1965 and the Circular 10/65 was not published until July, after it had been redrafted following consultation with the LEAs and teacher organizations.

The Circular made clear that it was the government's intention 'to end selection at 11+ and to eliminate separatism in secondary education'. Local authorities were requested to submit within a year plans for reorganization along comprehensive lines. The Circular did not, however, lay down a single form of organization. Instead, six different patterns — all of which were in operation in areas which had comprehensive schools — were offered for consideration. Of these six, all but patterns 5 and 6 below were regarded as suitable permanent patterns for the organization of comprehensive secondary schooling.

The six suggested patterns of organization were:

1 The single tier or 'all through' school catering for all children from the ages of 11 to 18.

2 A two-tier system whereby all children were transferred from a lower school to an upper school at age 13 or 14.

3 A two tier system comprising comprehensive schools for the age group 11–16 with sixth-form colleges offering education of the 16–18 age group. (It was envisaged that only a limited number of experiments would be allowed on this pattern).

4 A two-tier system comprising a middle school for all children aged 8–12 (or 9–13) and an upper school for the age range 12 (or 13) to 18. (Again the operation of this pattern would be strictly limited).

5 A two-tier system in which only those children who intended to sit public examinations transferred from junior to senior comprehensive school.

6 A two-tier system in which pupils were transferred at age 14 from a junior comprehensive school to two types of senior school, one catering for those who did not wish to stay in school beyond the statutory school leaving age and another type for those who did.

The introduction of comprehensive school reform by means of a Circular *requesting* local authorities to submit plans for comprehensive reorganization, rather than by means of legislation *compelling* local authorities to reorganize, indicates that the 'compulsion/cooperation' debate was ultimately resolved in favour of those within the party who had argued that a Labour government should not compel local authorities to reorganize. It is worth noting here that, if Crossman's recollections are accurate, the decision not to legislate to compel was the result of one of the few serious discussions of education policy in Cabinet during the years 1964–70 and was made with only minor dissent, although among the three dissenters was the stop-gap Education Secretary Michael Stewart.

From 1965 Until 1987 — Two Decades of Controversy

Between 1966 and 1970, when the Labour government lost office, the proportion of secondary age pupils at comprehensive schools went up from 12 per cent to 40 per cent, yet the arrival of a Conservative government in 1970 in which Margaret Thatcher withdrew Circular 10/65 and replaced it with Circular 10/70, thereby removing central government backing for comprehensivization, saw no slackening of the rate of growth of the comprehensive sector. By 1973, 50 per cent of all secondary pupils were in such schools and the return of a Labour government in 1974 generated Circular 4/74 which revived overt government backing for comprehensives of two types — 11–18 all-through schools and the tiered schools, where all pupils transferred at 13 or 14 from 'junior' secondary to 'senior' secondary schools.

The subsequent 1976 Education Act's introduction of compulsion through its prohibition that no maintained schools were to select with regard to ability or aptitude seems in most accounts (for example, Bellaby, 1976) to have had remarkably little effect in further speeding what was already a very rapid growth in the comprehensive sector — by 1977 80 per cent of state education pupils were in such schools.

However, the advent of the new Conservative government in 1979 seems to have slowed further progress. The 1976 Education Act was itself repealed in 1979, although the High Court and the Court of Appeal's decision in 1976 that Tameside LEA (which wanted to reintroduce selection) was not acting 'unreasonably' in the 1976 Act's meaning of the term had already made the Act itself of doubtful usefulness or strength. The appointment of Sir Keith Joseph as Education Minister in 1981 brought, as Shaw (1983) somewhat dramatically notes, 'the first minister who appears positively hostile to comprehensive schooling since Margaret Thatcher' and Joseph's ideology appeared to be reflected in an increased unwillingness to approve LEA comprehensivization plans where these threatened established grammar schools of good reputation or where vocal support was raised against them.

Since Joseph rejected only nineteen out of seventy-three LEA plans, (*Hansard*, 8 July 1986) the small growth in the comprehensive sector from 80 per cent of pupils in 1977 to only 83 per cent of pupils in 1981 seems likely to reflect changing levels of enthusiasm for the schools at LEA level. Given the historically decentralized nature of the British educational system Reynolds, 1984a), local government has possessed considerable autonomy in its choice of organizational structures and it seems likely that public expressions of concern about comprehensive school academic standards by Boyson, Joseph and others on the 'radical right' of the Conservative party may have had both direct effects on LEA opinion and indirect effects mediated through a mobilization of middle class voters that have combined to slow the move from selective education.

In some LEAs which have already gone comprehensive, in fact, there have been proposals to reintroduce some form of selection, such as the 'super grammar schools' proposed for Hereford and Worcestershire and for Solihull. In Redbridge, and in Cheltenham, by contrast proposals have merely been to re-establish the traditional 20 per cent of pupils in selective schools. Although the Solihull proposals were abandoned and, at the time of writing, those of the other LEAs seem unlikely to go forward, the sudden flurry of schemes to reintroduce the selective system perhaps stands to illustrate the tenuous hold that the comprehensive system has attained. Although Benn and Simon (1970) felt able to argue that, '... comprehensive education is now securely established in Britain' (p. 347), it is the *insecurity* of the comprehensive enterprise which is now most striking.

Why Comprehensive Schooling?

We have outlined so far the historical development of comprehensive school educational policy. This historical account left unresolved an issue which has exercised the minds of commentators and social scientists alike for many years, which is of explaining exactly *why* the Labour government implemented a policy of comprehensive education. The leadership of the Parliamentary Labour Party and the parliamentary party as a whole were scarcely notable in the decade following the end of World War II for their support of the reorganization of secondary schooling along comprehensive lines. Yet by 1964, and subsequently, the policy was presented in general election manifestoes as one of the vital policy planks of future Labour governments. How is this policy commitment — albeit in the nature of an eleventh hour repentance by some members of the Labour leadership — to be explained?

The existing literature on comprehensive school reform provides us with four possible, though not necessarily mutually exclusive, explanations:

(i)   That the Labour commitment — translated into political action by the issuing of Circular 10/65 — was the result of a long-term commitment by the Labour Party to promote social equality by means of the education system.

(ii) That Labour's comprehensive school reform was in large part a reaction to changing conceptions of social justice in British society.

(iii) That the adoption, development and implementation of a comprehensive school policy by the Labour party was a response to the growing body of research findings which questioned the scientific validity of the theory of general intelligence (which had been used to justify the establishment of the tripartite system after 1944) and demonstrated that the selective organization of secondary education had been responsible for a significant 'wastage of academic talent'.

(iv) That Labour's introduction of this educational reform reflected the coincidence at a point in time of support for comprehensivization by the representatives of organized 'capital' and organized 'labour'.

In the following pages we describe and discuss the arguments marshalled in support of the various explanations, attempt a critique of the first explanation offered and then attempt to synthesize and expand the other three explanations in a way which produces in our opinion the most accurate portrayal of the reasons why comprehensivisation emerged as government policy by the early 1960s and why Labour governments subsequently have been committed to the policy.

The Comprehensive School and Labour Party Egalitarianism

The first explanation for the adoption and implementation of a comprehensive school policy argues that the reform was the direct result of an adherence by the Labour Party to an ideology of egalitarianism and of a determination to promote social equality by means of the education system. Arguments used to support this explanation therefore eschew the possibility that factors outside the Labour Party may have had a significant influence on policy formulation and implementation.

This explanation is most forcibly proposed by some of the contributors to the so called *Black Papers on Education*. Maude (1969) in an article which discusses what he believes to be the 'egalitarian threat' to British society argues that the reasons for the adoption, development and implementation of the comprehensive school policy are to be found in Labour's stubborn adherence to egalitarian ideology — an ideology which, in his opinion, is antithetic to sound educational theory. Another contributor, Szamuely, propounds the view that the replacement of the tripartite system by the comprehensive system was advocated in order to effect not an improvement in academic skills but as 'the implementation of social change ... a means of breaking down the country's social structure and creating equality of opportunity'.

This direct link between the supposed egalitarian ideology of the Labour Party and the comprehensive school policy is discussed by Bilski (1971) in an article entitled 'Ideology and the Comprehensive School'. She argues that the policies of both the Labour and Conservative parties on comprehensive education were largely determined by their particular opposing ideologies. Both parties, in her opinion, used the arguments of the teaching profession and the evidence of research as mere supporting evidence and *only* when they were congruent with the moral principles on which Party ideology was based. In the case of the Labour Party, Bilski argues it was a commitment to egalitarian ideology which embraced the principles of fellowship and equality that led to the development and implementation of comprehensive school policy.

She supports this explanation by following the discussion over secondary education in the Labour Party through the years 1940–70. She picks up the debate in the years preceding the 1944 Education Act and explains Labour's support for the multilateral school during this period in terms of the, then still general, acceptance of individual differences and the overall immutability of levels of general intelligence. In this context the choice which was presented to the Labour party was the choice between support for a tripartite organization of secondary education which would segregate children socially and educationally at age 11 or support for a multilateral organization of secondary schooling which, whilst segregating children educationally, would facilitate social class mixing and equality of social status. The choice, Bilski suggests, was an easy one for Labour to make.

The development of the comprehensive school policy post-1944 was, according to Bilski, somewhat more complex and she characterizes this period as one in which there was a tension between the ideology of the party (an ideology of social egalitarianism expressed in support for the comprehensive school) and the official education policy of the Labour government (support for tripartism expressed by Wilkinson and Tomlinson). In the later years of this period the tension between policy and ideology was heightened by arguments in favour of the comprehensive school on grounds of educational equality. These arguments were based on indications from the small number of comprehensive schools established during this period that a wider range of pupils was capable of success in external examinations than a tripartite organisation of secondary education presupposed. Such *educational* evidence, according to Bilski was used to support Labour's commitment to comprehensives for their *social* effects.

In Labour's period of government from 1964 to 1970 evidence is provided, Bilski claims, that the 'weak' formulations on comprehensive schooling were merely politically expedient. Circular 10/65, she believes, makes it quite clear in its preference for the all-through school that the purely ideological comprehensive principle had remained sacred in Labour's thinking and Labour's willingness to prepare legislation to compel recalcitrant local authorities to reorganize in 1970 led her to believe that the circle had been finally closed and Labour egalitarian policy and ideology completely harmonized.

Similar arguments have been recently generated by Shaw's (1983) view of comprehensive education as a form of egalitarian conspiracy.

The Labour Party, Comprehensive Schools and Social Justice

If we characterize the first explanation of the implementation of a comprehensive school policy as one which proposes *purposive* ideological action by the Labour party as the reason for educational change then the second type of explanation can be characterized as one which sees the Labour Party as *reacting* to wider social changes. In general terms this second explanation suggests that the implementation of the policy should be seen as a response by the Labour party to changing societal conceptions of social justice.

There are two versions of this explanation. The first version sees the reform as the product of pressure exerted by the middle class section of the population — the second variant presents the reform as the result of a much more significant redefinition of the concept of social justice by a wider section of society, a redefinition which made it both imperative that academic differentiation should be delayed in order to facilitate equality of educational opportunity *and* that secondary education should be provided in a single school to reduce social class antagonisms.

An expression of the first explanation is to be found in the opening chapter of Ford's (1969) *Social Class and the Comprehensive School* where the author suggests that a redefinition of the concept of social justice in education took place among certain middle class parents. They were the parents of children who had in the late 1950s failed to gain access to grammar schools because a significant increase in the number of secondary school children had not been matched by an increase in the number of grammar school places available. The redefinition is said to have been the result of a process whereby a group which had traditionally been associated with high status educational provision and for whom that association had now been severed came to define themselves as 'relatively deprived'.

In consequence of this status inconsistency between the experience of low quality schooling and the membership of a highly aspiring and achieving social class, this group were driven to a redefinition of social justice in education which held that only a secondary system which offered to all children access to high quality education would satisfy the principle of social justice. Vocal middle class groups through their activities in pro-comprehensive school pressure groups and their traditional access to influential figures inside and outside government applied irresistible pressure on the Labour party to implement its policy commitment when it returned to power.

The second version of this thesis is most clearly presented in a speech delivered by the late Anthony Crosland in 1966 and reproduced in his volume of essays *Socialism Now* (1974). According to Crosland, the movement towards comprehensive education and its introduction whilst he was Secretary of State for Education reflected 'an irresistible pressure in British society to extend the rights of citizenship'. The introduction of comprehensive schooling is seen in the context of the constant redefinitions in the concept of social justice which had occurred over three centuries. These redefinitions had extended the rights of citizens first to personal liberty, then to democratic rights, then to social welfare and finally — through the comprehensive school reform — to educational equality. These redefinitions were in part the result of social struggles which ultimately applied irresistable pressure for change.

The factors contributing to this final redefinition of social justice are seen by Crosland as threefold. The first was the effect of sociological and psychological research evidence which as we mentioned earlier suggested that individual intelligence levels were a function of social environment as well as genetic endowment.

The second factor, which Crosland believed contributed to a redefinition of social justice in education, is also concerned with research evidence. In the late 1950s evidence became available which suggested that the system of allocation of children to one type of school or another in the tripartite system was seriously inaccurate. Such evidence, then, indicated that the system of selection at age 11 militated against any kind of educational justice and aided the redefinition of social justice in education.

Finally, such evidence as had become available suggested that social class divisions were exacerbated by the operation of a selective secondary school system. This was argued to be the case because selection at 11+ had the effect of selecting in large part middle class pupils for grammar school places and working class pupils for modern school places. As the result of selecting already socially privileged children for places in the high status grammar schools, the education system was said to be merely confirming social status and sharpening social class divisions.

In Crosland's explanation of comprehensive reform, then, the rationale and dynamic for change is argued to be a redefinition — by society as a whole — of the concept of social justice. This redefinition itself is seen as part of a continuous process of extending the rights of citizens and prescribed an education system which attempted to ensure as far as possible equality of educational opportunity, parity of social prestige and the diminution of social class antagonisms.

Education, the Economy and the Comprehensive Principle

The third theory of educational change proposes that the transformation of Labour's comprehensive policy into government action should be seen primarily as a response to economic and technological factors. Government and private research had in the period leading up to 1965 demonstrated not only that long held theories of the nature of intelligence were invalid but also that the continuance of the tripartite system would have serious and detrimental effects on the development of the British economy. During the 1950s and 1960s rapid technological development was occurring throughout the world and it seemed obvious to economic planners, farsighted politicians and academics that only the nation which embraced 'the white heat of the technological revolution' would gain economic stability and development. However, rapid technological advance would produce a demand for a larger reservoir of skilled workers and technicians which research seemed to indicate could not be satisfied by the existing divided system of secondary education. As early as 1959 the Crowther Report warned:

> The average worker in industry requires much more education than was needed only a short time ago.
> ... The growth in the proportion of highly skilled jobs and the decline in the proportion of unskilled jobs imply a reassessment of what must be attempted by people of only average intelligence.
> ... It is not only at the top but almost to the bottom of the pyramid that the scientific revolution of our times needs to be reflected in a longer educational process.

The tripartite system (or bipartite as it had evolved because few technical secondary schools had been established) had ensured that, for the most part, only basic skills were taught in the secondary modern schools. In fact, until the late 1950s the teaching of subjects to public examination level in these schools was virtually unheard of. Britain, then, in the late 1950s was ill equipped with talent to capitalize on the technological and scientific changes which were taking place.

The consequences of a realization of such a lack of talent were according to this theory of change twofold: firstly, many secondary modern schools evolved more academic curricula and entered more pupils in public examinations in an attempt to satisfy the need for a larger pool of ability; secondly, the realization provided the basic dynamic and rationale for a reform of the secondary school system which would yield an organizational form capable of maximizing the talent available and enlarging the pool of pupils with high levels of skills.

Capital, Labour and the Comprehensive School

So far, then, we have outlined three explanations of educational change. The first explanation proposes that the comprehensive education reform should be seen as resulting from the supposed dominant egalitarian ideology of the Labour party. The second and third explanations suggest a more or less consensual move from one form of secondary system to another, necessitated by changes in the concept of social justice and/or by technological change.

In contrast to all three of these explanations, those writers whose political and philosophical orientation is Marxist claim that the development of comprehensive school policy and its implementation owes more to a process of struggle than to a consensual societal process. Change in the provision and structure of education over time is often interpreted as change which is potentially advantageous to the interests of 'labour' or 'capital' (for example, Simon, 1974). Such changes reflect the outcome at any one time of the struggle between the capitalist and working classes but they may also reflect the ability of the capitalist class — when such changes are politically progressive and therefore apparently advantageous to the working class — to adapt its strategy in order to subvert such potentially progressive changes. If this analysis is followed, the process of educational change this century might be explained as follows.

Before 1944 the system of private secondary education mirrored the social structure of British society by restricting access to secondary education to those children whose parents could afford such education — the middle and upper classes. As the education system restricted high status education to children who had been associated with high status occupations, it did little more than confirm social status. However, as a result of pressure from the labour and trade union movement, and of the resolve of the political agents of the ruling class to make concessions in education rather than in other more important areas, the 1944 Act provided for a system of secondary education available free of charge to all children over the age of 11. On the one hand, the Act can be interpreted as a victory for the Labour movement and its allies who had campaigned long and hard for the introduction of free education available to all. On the other hand, the victory can be seen as pyrrhic on two counts. Firstly, it might be argued that it was a victory won at the cost of a more extensive victory and, secondly, it might be held that the organizational form which secondary education took and the failure to make a greater number of grammar school places available to the early years of the new system ensured that access to high status education was still largely restricted to the sons and daughters of a social elite.

Similarly, according to Simon (1978) the comprehensive school reform might be seen as a twin-edged victory. In the years between 1944 and 1965 the Labour movement and other left wing and progressive forces had campaigned for a reorganization of secondary education along comprehensive lines. In 1965 the Labour government apparently acceded to this pressure but the actual reorganization of secondary education — if in part effected by the movement for comprehensive education — can also be seen as a change which could equally well be utilized in the interests of the capitalist class as in the interests of the bulk of the population. This is so because whilst Circular 10/65 encouraged reorganization, it in no way prescribed the internal academic organization of the comprehensive school and some of the optional schemes outlined in the Circular can be seen as facilitating academic selection. If the new comprehensive schools were to continue the process of academic selection, comprehensive education might be seen as having positive *advantages* for the capitalist class. The new schools might produce a larger pool of ability because mistakes in academic selection would not be reinforced as in the old system by organizational barriers, whilst still confirming the status of a social and educational elite. It is not difficult, if one follows this analysis, to conceive of comprehensive reorganizations as the result of a strange coincidence of support for some kind of change in secondary education from both organized labour and organised capital.

Another Marxist writer, Bellaby (1976), expands and develops this hypothesis of coincidental support. He suggests that there are two sets of factors which explain the introduction of comprehensive schooling in 1965. The first set of factors is the interests of the capitalist class in retaining control over the labour force and the second set of factors is the interests and values of groups within the British labour force whose position has been altered by changes in the structure of capitalism.

According to this explanation the impetus for comprehensive reform came in part from within capitalism. Instead of resorting (as entrepreneurial capitalism had) to coercive and repressive means of controlling the labour force, the modern capitalism of state and multi-national private companies solves the problem of order in society by setting one section of the labour force against another. The comprehensive school is seen as contributing to the solution of the problem of order by providing an education system in which all pupils feel themselves to be part of the same community whilst social inequalities are covertly reproduced by the continued existence of academic selection procedures which have the effect of rewarding adjudged academic ability. Such a system of education was, according to Bellaby, seen by the capitalist class in mid-twentieth century Britain as having the dual merits of socializing all children into an advanced labour process and of preventing them from developing a single anti-capitalist political consciousness.

In contrast, those representatives of labour who had been involved in the movement for educational reform had long-term interests which were diametrically opposed to the interests of 'capital'. Nevertheless, suggests Bellaby, modern capitalism had developed to a point in the post-war period where the majority of the population formed 'the battalion of labour' and such developments had paradoxically caused the interests of capital and labour to coincide in the field of education. Indeed, the comprehensive school idea seemed to offer advantages to all sections of post-war British society: for the working class it appeared to offer the opportunity — through educational achievement — of social mobility; for the new middle class the consumption of education seemed a valuable insurance policy against the vulnerability inherent in their intermediate position between the working class and the capitalist class; for teachers in low status secondary modern schools which had not achieved parity of esteem and resource allocation with the grammar schools, the comprehensive school held out the opportunity of greater status and career advancement. Each of these sections of the population were therefore united in a common educational purpose and formed the nucleus of a vocal and influential movement for comprehensive education. This movement, in turn, impressed on the Labour party both the electoral attraction of a comprehensive school policy and the irresistible momentum of the demand for the implementation of such a policy.

There are, then, four main types of explanation of Labour's commitment to, and adoption of, a policy of comprehensive reorganization of the secondary school system. Having described each of these explanations, we wish to suggest in the following pages that none of the theories outlined provide a complete explanation of the reasons for Labour's adoption of the policy in 1965, and we wish to go on to outline our own explanation for why comprehensive schooling became Government policy.

The Labour Party, Egalitarianism and the Comprehensive Issue — A 'Red Herring'

As we have seen, the first type of explanation — promoted by Shaw, Bilski and some of the Black Paper writers — suggests that the comprehensive school reform was the product of a commitment by the Labour party to the ideology of egalitarianism. According to this explanation, the comprehensive school reform was introduced in order to create an education system which promoted social equality, the dissolution of the existing social structure and socialist political change. There are, we believe, three major weaknesses in the evidence and arguments developed by the proponents of this type of theory:

(i)   The explanation rests upon an analysis of the Labour party which suggests a general ideological homogeneity which is in reality conspicuous by its absence.

(ii) The explanation minimises the extent of ideological divergence on this particular issue within the Labour party.

(iii) The explanation assumes a degree of commitment to egalitarian policies by the Labour party which is simply unwarranted by the available evidence.

The Shaping and Introduction of the Comprehensive Policy — A New Synthesis

It is, however, our belief that none of the other explanations we described earlier in the chapter provide anything more than partial accounts of why Labour's leaders and parliamentary members supported the introduction of a comprehensive school policy as government policy. There is quite clear evidence that the late 1950s saw public dissatisfaction with the system of academic selection at 11 and there seems to be some evidence that Labour's leaders of the time were acutely aware of the pressure expressed by parents of children who had been dispossessed of the grammar school places that were traditionally theirs. It also seems likely that both the social democratic majority within the Parliamentary party and the parliamentary leadership in the years leading up to 1965 would have been influenced by Crosland's support of comprehensive schooling on the basis of an argument concerned with the rights of citizens to be socially equal in a democratic society. The welter of research showing the inaccuracy of the instrument of academic selection at age 11, the inability of the tripartite system to generate talent and the under-representation of intelligent working class children in the grammar schools seem also to have had some considerable influence on the leadership of a party avowedly attempting to marry the twin concerns of increased social justice with the increased generation of wealth by a capitalist economy.

The multiplicity of patterns of education for comprehensive schooling sanctioned by Crosland in Circular 10/65 might also be regarded as giving some support to the Marxist analysis of the forces at play. The traditional egalitarian cry of the political left for comprehensive schooling was supplemented by the cries of the capitalist class for a changed system of education which would generate a more talented workforce to cater for the needs of technological and economic change, and also was supplemented by the support of disappointed middle class parents and secondary modern school teachers. The Labour government, in adopting a policy of comprehensive education, sought to give the appearance of satisfying the aspirations of the left, but in granting a large degree of freedom in the academic and social organization of comprehensive schools it precluded the possibility of a unified *socialist* system of secondary education. In facilitating greater flexibility in academic selection (though not precluding selection per se), Labour's plans also appear to have facilitated the picking of a greater number of educational 'winners' and, by situating all children of one area in one school, to have fostered social equality among pupils. In so doing, Labour's plans could be regarded as reflecting the demands of capital. In making one school out of two or three, Labour of course also satisfied the social status aspirations of 'dispossessed' middle class children and stigmatized secondary modern school teachers.

The picture which we believe unfolds is of a parliamentary leadership and party reactively and gradually realizing that a policy which had its original roots in an egalitarian ideology was amenable to modification into a policy form which was congruent both with social democratic ideology and also with popular electoral appeal. Consequently the party leadership, many of whom had been explicitly or silently hostile to comprehensive education in the late 1940s and early 1950s, redefined and tailored the comprehensive school policy so that it correlated with the dominant concerns of the largely social democratic Labour party of the late 1950s and early 1960s. These concerns, summarized below, seem to have close associations with the redefinition of the comprehensive school policy:

1   The period of Gaitskell's leadership of the Labour party saw the emergence of a coherent and well argued social democratic philosophy and strategy within the Labour Party. As we have indicated in earlier sections of this chapter this outlook argued that democratic and economic equality had largely been achieved in Britain. These peaceful democratic and economic 'revolutions' had effected a redistribution of power and financial resources. Consequently, according to this social democratic perspective, the Labour party needed no longer to be preoccupied with the nationalization of industry nor the winning of political power for working people. Instead Labour's policy thinking should be directed towards the evolution of policies which would remove the final societal evil, the evil of differential social *status*. One way of tackling this problem was, according to this group, through a reorganized education system which universalized access to a single educational institution at secondary level. In such a system academic achievement would reflect ability rather than social class and the removal of stratification between different types of school would ensure parity of social esteem for intelligent and less intelligent pupils. These concepts of *equality of educational opportunity* and *parity of social status* are evident in Gaitskell and Crosland's early definitions of comprehensive schooling and are quite clearly domi-

nant in both the official Labour commitments of 1958 and 1959 and in Harold Wilson's (1965) statements of support for comprehensive schooling in 1963 and 1964. Implicit in these official statements of support for comprehensive schooling is a commitment not to the egalitarian ideal of the abolition of academic selection and the fostering of social change but to the social democratic and Fabian expedients of increased meritocracy through the removal of permanent selection at age 11 and increased harmony between social classes by means of social mixing in the school.

2   During this period also Fabian social democracy appears to have been obsessed with the notion of a scientific revolution which through the generation of greater national wealth would further improve the living standards of the British people. Socialism, for the influential social democratic thinkers within the Labour party became defined as a process of profit generating technological change. However, as we have mentioned earlier, academic and government sponsored research produced findings which demonstrated that the tripartite system of education was unequal to the task of producing the diversity and quantity of talent which would make the dream of a new industrial revolution a reality. Gradually the Parliamentary party and the leadership came to embrace the comprehensive form of education as a means of producing, through the relaxation of the previous organizational barriers which were inhibiting to the maximization of talent, a battalion of well educated, technologically adaptable labour. The effect of the marriage of this vision of talent generation to the idea of equality of educational opportunity can be clearly seen in Harold Wilson's '*Science and Socialism*' speech to the 1963 Labour party conference and in his chapter on the subject in *The Relevance of Socialism* (1965) and is quite congruent with the portrayal of comprehensive education as 'grammar schools for all'. The transformation of the comprehensive ideal from the egalitarian ideal of its early group of supporters into the talent generating expedient of the parliamentary leadership of the later 1950s and early 1960s rested in part on the parliamentary leadership's ability in this period to gain acceptance for a social democratic definition of the concepts of equality and socialism.

3   In addition, we believe that commitment to support comprehensive reorganization along the redefined lines when Labour formed a government was influenced by evidence in the late 1950s which showed that, whilst there was growing dissatisfaction with permanent academic selection at age 11 amongst the general population, the dissatisfaction was expressed as a vote against the secondary modern schools rather than for a comprehensive system and also by evidence in the early 1960s which showed that the resultant policy was extremely attractive to the electorate. The adoption of the compre-

hensive school policy by the Labour party in its 1964 General Election manifesto was partially to gain votes.

Labour's 1964 comprehensive school policy therefore had the virtue for its leaders of apparently satisfying all the groups who had called for the comprehensive reorganization of secondary schooling and at the same time having the potential functional value of aiding a greater degree of harmony between social classes in a capitalist economy and generating a greater amount of talent to transform that capitalist economy into a successful generator of greater national wealth. With the internal organization of the schools left unspecified, all groups could agree on the framework. With goals of equal opportunity and more talent, even egalitarians could agree on the schools as a first step towards what they wanted.

Conclusions

In this chapter we have attempted to describe the rise of the comprehensive school as official government policy, to indicate the controversy that still surrounds the schools in the mid-1980s and lastly to analyze the reasons *why* comprehensivization emerged as an educational policy.

We have agreed that comprehensive schools were never seen by the Labour governments of the past as being 'egalitarian' institutions designed to equalize outcomes as between different children. As other commentators have noted (for example, Marsden, 1971), the Labour party has always adopted a 'weak' definition of comprehensive education that simply saw it as a more efficient and effective institution for generating children with unequal qualifications. A number of factors seem to have *predisposed* the party to adopt comprehensivization — the research evidence on wastage of ability in the selective system, combined with the influence of social democratic thinking, led to a desire to improve mechanisms of selection of pupils to increase equality of opportunity. Socialism's concern in the 1960s with the harnessing of science to generate wealth led to a concern to generate more talent and ability from amongst Britain's children. A concern for a more unified, harmonious social system led to desire for a more unified schooling system.

Whilst these factors predisposed governmental action, what seems to have *precipitated* that action was the political appeal of a comprehensive school policy, particularly one that could portray the new schools as giving to all the opportunities and traditions that had formerly been restricted to a few. Dissatisfaction with the secondary modern school could be assuaged, yet the high status of grammar school education could be retained and expanded through the ability range, as the tradition was handed on to pupils formerly denied it.

A local headteacher spelt out precisely this rationale for comprehensivization in a letter to *The Times* on 3 June 1978:

As a former headmaster proud of his own outstanding grammar school, I am second to none in my admiration of the debt the nation owes to the Welsh grammar schools.

However, I am now headmaster of a new purpose built, coeducational, 11–18 years comprehensive school. During the period of this school's existence, I can compare achievements and I claim that in the academic sense I am doing *more* not less for our most able pupils. We have a galaxy of teams involved in all manner of games and sports; we have bands, orchestras, choirs and dramatic productions; we have an enormous variety of extra-curricular clubs and societies. The standard of uniform is as high as in my former grammar school. The children are in the great majority courteous, well ordered and hard-working. My parents have an excellent association. The team spirit and morale of my staff room colleagues are high. What have I done to deserve such a school?

We are achieving this not only for the 25 per cent (or less) of the age group who would have gone to a selective grammar school. We are spreading all the benefits which the 25 per cent once enjoyed across the entire ability range in a comprehensive intake.

John Herbert,
Liswerry High School

The 'spreading' of the grammar school tradition that the headteacher refers to is, we believe, the key to understanding Labour policy on comprehensives, the nature of the schools themselves and the schools' inability to attain the goals that have been posited for them.

Chapter 2

The Effectiveness of Comprehensive Schooling

There are deficiencies in all existing comparative studies of school outcomes.   (Harvey Goldstein)

In chapter 1 we have described the development and implementation of comprehensive school policy. We have suggested that in proposing the comprehensive reorganization of secondary education, the 1964–70 Labour government was concerned primarily that such a reorganized system would generate high levels of academic attainment, especially in scientific and technological subjects which would service a technological economy, from a broader section of the ability range. We have also suggested that while this concern may be regarded as what predisposed the Labour government into political action on the issue, a more 'socialist' concern that the operation of the tripartite system was merely confirming individuals existing social status rather than reflecting their academic merit should be regarded as one of the more important factors which predisposed the Labour government to act. If our analysis is correct, another important factor predisposing action was a concern that the tripartite system's confirmation of the existing social status of its pupils, documented by research in the 1950s, acted to reinforce pupil perceptions of a rigid and fixed social class structure. Political factors *precipitated* policy action on the issue. Accordingly the criteria on which the operation of the comprehensive system should be judged, at least as far as its originators in Labour governments should be concerned, seem to be a three-fold focus:

1   A success of the comprehensive system in generating more academic attainment especially in scientific and technological subjects (i.e. more talent).
2   A success of the comprehensive system in aiding the growth of a meritocratic society in which ability rather than social class became a more powerful determinant of academic attainment (i.e. equality of opportunity).
3   A success of the comprehensive system in facilitating the social

mixing of children of different social classes, the breakdown of pupil perceptions of the social class structure as rigid and the replacement of such perceptions by perceptions of the wider society as flexible and hierarchical (i.e. more communality in pupil attitudes).

This chapter falls into two sections. In the first section we review the evidence which looks at the influence of the comprehensive system on pupil academic development and social development in Britain. In the second section, the very recent evidence on these issues is reviewed. We will follow the convention of presenting the evidence, reviewing possible defects and weaknesses in it and then at the end of each section assessing what the balance of evidence suggests to us about the relative effectiveness of the comprehensive system in attaining the above three goals.

The Effects of the Comprehensive System on Academic and Social Development

1   Academic Development

The evidence which seeks to assess the effect of the comprehensive system on academic development falls into three categories: studies which compare national academic standards over time; studies of examination results nationally and locally; and studies which assess the academic performance of comprehensive and selective systems of education on other measures of academic attainment.

Reading standards over time

Periodic investigations into the standard of reading have been one of the foci of debate over whether comprehensive education is improving or damaging national academic standards. The apparent decline in the reading standards of 11-year-old children in 1970/71 (Start and Wells, 1972) signalled a re-newed attack by Black Paper writers on 'creeping egalitarianism' in British education, progressive primary school teaching methods and comprehensive schooling (Cox and Boyson, 1977). It is difficult to understand the logic by which a supposed decline in reading standards amongst 11-year-olds was laid at the door of comprehensive schools whose pupils enter at 11+, (unless the very existence of a supposedly less rigorous secondary education sector is held to depress the performance of primary school teachers), but it is important to review the evidence on standards of reading for adolescents over time because so much attention has been given to the argument that academic standards have fallen as comprehensives have increased in number.

Since 1948 periodic surveys of the reading standards of 11 and 15-year-old children have been made using two reading tests, the Watts Vernon reading test and the NS6 reading test. The results of these surveys of reading ability suggest a consistent improvement in standards of reading comprehension from 1948 to the early 1960s. The 1970/71 test results, however, not only suggested that there had been a slight decline in reading standards since 1960/61 for 15-year-olds but also suggested that 11-year-old reading scores had declined by over four months since 1964 (Start and Wells, 1972).

The evidence concerning levels of illiteracy and semi-literacy over time is similarly difficult to interpret. Start and Wells (1972) suggest a sharp decline in illiteracy and semi-literacy in the thirty or so years prior to 1971. WD Wall (1945) had suggested that in the immediate pre-war years 10 per cent of children left school semi-literate and 1 per cent left school illiterate — a child was deemed to be semi-literate if he or she could not read to the standard of a 9-year-old child in 1938 and illiterate if he or she could not read to the mean 7-year-old standard. By comparison, Start and Wells show that the results of the 1970/71 national survey indicate that only 3 per cent of 15-year-old children were semi-literate and a negligible proportion illiterate (using 1938 definitions). However, this picture is not supported by other evidence — Start and Wells show that the semi-literacy level for 11-year-olds decreased from 25 per cent of children in 1948 to 13 per cent of 11-year-olds in 1964 but had increased to over 15 per cent in 1970. For 15-year-olds the rate appears to have declined from 6 per cent to negligible proportions between 1948 and 1964, but to have increased to 3 per cent in 1970.

The work of Cyril Burt also suggested a deterioration over time in standards of reading between 1914 and 1965 (see Wright, 1977 for a summary). The figures used purport to show a substantial decline between 1930 and 1940, with a slow recovery since then. The lack of representative samples of children, the fact that tested children had been selected by their teachers and the social changes in the inner London area over the period in question make the data — even if it were collected — to be in one authority's words 'meaningless' (Choppin, 1985, p. 95)

We have rather better information upon primary school reading standards from the periodic surveys of reading conducted by means of the NS6 reading test. Although there has been variation in the sampled and tested population and criticism as to whether the test has a high enough ceiling to tap the able children, mean standards have been slowly rising (Budge, 1986; Choppin, 1985). However, since these results are on primary school children, their relevance to the debate on the effects of comprehensive schools is somewhat marginal.

More recent Assessment of Performance Unit data upon 11 and 15-year-olds' reading and writing ability present a more optimistic assessment of trends than Start and Wells and concur with the above assertions of a modest improvement in performance. The recently published report of the 1979–1983 English language writing surveys noted that there was '. . . no evidence of illiteracy . . . no collapse of standards was discovered . . . secondary performance remained stable' (APU, quoted in Budge, 1986, p. 13). The

1979–1983 reading surveys analysis (about to be published at the time of writing) also suggests a small improvement in the reading standards of 15-year-olds.

Drawing conclusions from this mass of conflicting evidence is a very difficult task. The evidence suggests, in our view and that of Rutter (1980), that significant improvements in the average reading standards of 15-year-olds might have been followed by a plateau or slight decline in the early to mid-1970s. This may well have been followed by a slight improvement in the late 1970s and early 1980s, although whether this outweighs the decline reported by Start and Wells and the slight decline noted by Rodgers' (1984) recent analysis of data from the MRC health and development cohort is somewhat unclear.

Numerical standards over time

The astounding feature of national surveys of numeracy over time is their absence. Though educationists and the general public are treated to liberal doses of despondency (especially from employers) about the numerical standards of school leavers, there is hardly a shred of evidence which produces support or opposition to the now commonly-held view that numerical skills are in decline. What evidence exists is scrappy and incidental. A test conducted by the BBC *Man Alive* programme in 1977, with the assistance of the NFER, suggested that the performance of 14-year-olds in mathematics had declined sharply since 1964 (Hopkins, 1979). On the other hand, the proportion of school leavers obtaining a pass in 'O' level mathematics rose consistently in the years 1952 to 1984 according to DES statistics, although the rate of increase has been somewhat slower since 1974.

What is to be made of these figures? Very little, we suspect. The *Man Alive* survey was carried out using a very small sample and the growth in the pass rate in 'O' level mathematics may reflect differences in entry policy or pass standards for external examinations over time.

Recent APU analysis of its mathematics surveys from 1979 to 1983 suggests (Budge, 1986) a slight improvement of approximately 1½ per cent in average performance at mathematics over that period.

Overall, as with the reading scores, it is difficult to say whether comprehensivization has improved or retarded standards of numeracy. There is simply not enough evidence to justify a conclusion, except to say that any change is likely to have been highly marginal.

Examination results over time

A frequent claim of writers hostile to the theory and practice of comprehensive education is that these schools have lowered levels of academic attainment over time (Baldwin, in Cox and Boyson, 1977).

A preliminary look at the basic statistics on this matter suggests the contrary. These show that (DES, 1986; Rutter, 1980):

(i)   the proportion of leavers with no graded result fell from 44 per cent in 1970/71 to 18.7 per cent in 1975/76 and to 12.2 per cent in 1983/84;

(ii) the proportion of leavers gaining five or more 'higher grade' 'O' level or CSE passes rose from 20 per cent in 1964/65 to almost 27 per cent in 1983/84.

Unfortunately, the interpretation that the above evidence provides support for the case that comprehensive schools have raised academic attainment is not as clear cut as might first appear. There are six specific objections which can be raised against this interpretation. The first concerns the question of equivalency of a good 'O' level pass and a CSE grade 1 pass and some have argued that the increase in higher grade pass rates may have been contributed to, in part, by the addition of grade 1 results in an 'easier' examination. The second objection relates to the improvement in the rate of pupils achieving one or more middle grade 'O' level or higher grade CSE. In this case arguments about equivalency are supplemented by evidence that whilst the rate of success may have risen, it did so largely because a growing number of pupils (nearly 50 per cent in 1978) offered only one or two 'O' level or CSE papers for examination. A third objection is raised to an interpretation of a drop in the proportion of pupils achieving no examination passes as meaning that academic standards have necessarily risen. This claim would only be substantiated, some say, if a pass at a lower grade in CSE, or a pass at CSE Mode III, had any academic value, the likelihood of which they doubt. A fourth doubt about the validity of the evidence relates to the possibility of double counting. A pupil in an English comprehensive school where 'O' level and CSE examinations are held on different days could, hypothetically, be entered by his or her school in five subjects at 'O' level and the same five subjects at CSE. If that pupil were then to gain grade 1 passes in all subjects he/she was entered for at 'O' and CSE level, he/she would be counted twice as achieving five higher grade 'O' levels and five CSE grade 1s and would therefore artificially inflate the pass rate. The fifth objection to regarding the pass rate information as demonstrating an improvement in academic standards is that examinations may over time have become easier to pass, since the academic standard expected of a pupil passing may have been lowered. This objection is seemingly given support by a study carried out by Wilmott (1977) of CSE and GCE pass rates in the years 1968 and 1973. Wilmott matched examinees for CSE examinations in 1968 and 1973 on the basis of their IQ and found that children of similar measured IQ were getting higher grades at CSE in 1973 than their counterparts in 1968. He calculated that CSE standard had 'slipped' by a third of a grade in the intervening five years. The sixth objection raised is that the increased pass rates may simply reflect changes in the examination entry policy of schools. Children who have hitherto not been entered for examinations may be entered for some and may pass some.

How valid are these objections and do they seriously cast into doubt the apparent upward trend of academic attainments? Let us look briefly at each of the objections in turn and evaluate their validity. First, the claim that no meaningful equivalency exists between the good 'O' level pass and the CSE grade 1 pass. This objection, though frequently made, is based on no empirical evidence and should, therefore, be regarded as unproven. The objection that the pass rate of pupils gaining one or more middle grade 'O' levels or higher grade CSEs is artificially inflated by a large number of pupils who offer only one or two subjects for examination is similarly difficult to evaluate. If one accepts the *prima facie* case that the pass rate of pupils obtaining high grade qualifications has increased and that the proportion of pupils obtaining no qualifications has decreased, then it is difficult to escape the conclusion that the large section of pupils who offer only one or two subjects for examination are drawn from that section of the school population which were either entered for no examinations or gained no passes.

This would lead one to suspect that the figures actually indicate an increased *depth* of the examination pool rather than a *depression* of standards. The difficulty is of course that such an interpretation rests on the basis of other similarly challenged data and we can therefore do little more than judge that the assertion that standards have been artificially inflated is no more solidly based than the opposite assertion. The third objection is like the first more an assertion than an objection, perhaps based on employers' refusal to accept CSE passes — and especially passes in Mode III — as academically meaningful. The problem of 'double counting' is of course a valid problem. The assessment that needs to be made is whether such double counting contributes significantly to improvement in the pass rate at 'O' level/CSE. We are unable to assess with any certainty the significance of this but it seems extremely unlikely that it would constitute a significant factor in the calculation of passes. Wilmott's study seems to present the strongest evidence that an increase in the proportion of pupils gaining certificates does not necessarily correlate with an improvement in academic standards. However, this study has been the subject of severe criticism. Wilmott's matching of pupils was achieved by the use of a standard reference test to indicate IQ level but a number of examining boards claimed the test to be hopelessly inaccurate. Wilmott's assumption that examination marking has become more lenient is based on findings which show a tendency for IQ scores to be getting lower but for examination grades to be remaining constant. This assumption is made, however, without consideration of the possibility that there was a change in the population base between 1968 and 1973, a possibility which, as Rutter (1980, p. 114) notes, is 'immediately raised by the substantial drop in mean IQ between 1968 and 1973' and which is almost certainly a 'consequence of the very great rise in the number of children taking GCE and CSE examinations at 16 years'. The implication is that as examinations have become more available to less able candidates, the level of ability of candidates will have fallen accordingly. Sampling for the study was by school and not by individual, which is important because of the rising number of children leaving school to do GCE and CSE in colleges of further education. Finally, the study is flawed because correlations between IQ and examination scores vary widely by subject. In consequence of these powerful criticisms, it appears necessary to conclude that Wilmott's claims are unsubstantiated by the results of his study. The sixth objection, whilst it may in substance be correct, constitutes not an argument that recent changes masquerade as improvements in standards but that previous entry policy artificially depressed attainments.

Doubts as to Willmott's suggestions that higher numbers of children passing may simply be due to lower criteria of what a pass necessitates are also cast by the Christie and Forrest study of standards in 'A' level marking over time. Although it must be remembered that the authors saw this as a feasibility study rather than a substantive piece of work in its own right, their re-marking of the 1963 and 1973 Joint Matriculation Board scripts suggested that whilst there had been a negligible shift downwards in mathematics standards at 'A' level, this was balanced by a tightening in English standards (cited in Budge, 1986).

Our conclusion in this section analyzing comprehensive school effects upon academic development over the course of the 1960s, 1970s and 1980s can only emphasize again the extreme difficulty of drawing any definitive conclusions. Over these years there have been major social and economic changes that have created a social climate perhaps much more hostile to educational goals than before — if levels of academic development have not improved, that may reflect these outside-school factors and not the changes wrought by comprehensivisation.

Overall, though, we suspect that the evidence suggests very limited effects of the change to comprehensives upon pupil development. Levels of reading ability seem to have improved, dipped and improved again. Levels of numeracy are impossible to assess. Improvements in examination passes and in the qualifications of school leavers *may* have taken place on a modest scale. If comprehensives have failed or improved standards, the evidence suggests that they have probably had a marginal and very limited effect.

Comprehensive versus selective — comparisons of academic attainment rates at a point in time

Over the last thirty years there have been a proliferation of research studies which have attempted to assess the relative effectiveness of the comprehensive and the selective systems in promoting the academic development of their pupils. Some of these studies compare national rates of examination success in the two systems whilst some compare the success rates in examinations of a sample of schools from the selective system with a sample of schools from the comprehensive system. Still others compare the two systems on measures of academic attainment other than public examination results. In this section we will review in chronological order studies of all the above types.

Koshe (1957) studied the academic attainment levels of third form pupils in a grammar school, two comprehensive schools and two secondary modern schools, using measures of intelligence, ability in English and ability in arithmetic. His findings suggested that the comprehensive school boys possessed ability in arithmetic superior to that of boys in the modern schools, that boys in one of the two comprehensive schools had superior arithmetic scores to boys in the grammar school, that girls in both comprehensive schools achieved superior scores to girls in the modern schools on all three measures of attainment, that girls in one of the comprehensive schools were better than the girls in the grammar school on the arithmetic test and that the grammar school girls gained higher scores than girls in the comprehensive schools on the IQ and English tests. A number of points need to be borne in mind in interpreting these findings. Firstly, the comprehensive schools in the study did not receive the full ability range of the areas in which they were situated since they were creamed. Secondly, the sample is drawn from a small number of schools. Finally, there is no attempt to present comparative findings for all pupils of both sexes. It is difficult in consequence to gain a clear picture of the relative success of each of the systems. The fact that the comprehensive schools in the study were essentially secondary modern schools with an added selective stream might lead one to conclude that the comprehensive schools were performing favourably when compared to the selective schools which had the full range of ability. On the other hand, the use of an intelligence measure as the sole indicator of ability on which pupils in one system were matched with pupils in the other throws some doubt on whether the study compared like with like. Whilst IQ has a high correlation with mathematical ability the correlation is much lower with ability in English.

In a study of pass rates in comprehensive schools and selective schools in East Sussex during the years 1959–61, Pedley (1969) discovered that whilst 10 per cent of school leavers gained a 'good GCE result' in the selective system as a whole over this period, the rate for comprehensive schools in the area was 18 per cent. Again, however, the study has important weaknesses: Pedley had no measures of academic intake quality into the two systems which would demonstrate whether comparisons were being made of school populations with similar levels of ability, neither does he present any information about the examination entry policy of the comprehensive and selective schools. If it was the case in this study, as seems likely, that the comprehensive schools entered a greater proportion of their pupils for examinations, then one would expect this to have depressed the overall pass rate. If this is the case, the absence of intake data for the two systems notwithstanding, Pedley's East Sussex comprehensive schools appear to have been performing extraordinarily well.

In 1964–65 Pedley carried out a further survey of GCE examination results in comprehensive schools which had been established between 1945 and 1955. From an 80 per cent return to this survey, he found that twenty-four schools could be defined as fully comprehensive by his criteria: that a school be deemed fully comprehensive if it recruited practically all local children and that any losses to grammar or independent schools did not exceed 5 per cent of the age group. When the 'O' and 'A' level performance of these twenty-four schools for the academic year 1962/63 was compared with that of all maintained schools in England and Wales the following results emerged:

Table 1: Percentage of school leavers

| | GCE 'O' level passes | | 2 or more |
	1 or more (%)	5 or more (%)	GCE 'A' level passes (%)
All maintained schools, England and Wales	26	13	5.3
Twenty-four early comprehensive schools (3610 leavers)	32	16	7.5

Once more, Pedley's comprehensive schools appear to be performing considerably better than the national average. Once more, however, the results may well be misleading. As the study can offer no indication of the academic intake quality of the twenty-four comprehensives relative to that of the maintained system as a whole it would be unwise to conclude that Pedley is necessarily comparing like with like. Furthermore, Pedley's twenty-four comprehensive schools are drawn largely from rural areas in the North, West and Midlands of England. As such the schools may well be atypical in the higher intake quality of their pupils. Whilst Pedley attempts to deal with this problem by asserting that the regional statistics for the areas in which the schools are situated show that the areas do less well in examinations than the South of England, this does not resolve the problem in any way as regional statistics cover heterogeneous areas. Perhaps the most charitable assessment of this study is that Pedley does not prove that comprehensive schools are better promoters of academic talent than the selective system.

No doubt heartened by his earlier findings Pedley conducted a further survey in 1968/69. This time he collected data on the public examination performance of sixty-seven established comprehensive schools, representing a 73 per cent response rate to his enquiries, for the academic year 1967/68. He found that his comprehensive schools yielded the following results: 39.4 per cent of all leavers gained at least one 'O' level pass or CSE grade 1 pass; 20.1 per cent achieved five or more 'O' levels or CSE grade 1 passes; and 9.7 per cent of all leavers gained two or more 'A' level passes. Whilst these figures compare favourably with results in the maintained system as a whole, this study too has been subject to severe criticisms. The study has been criticized on the grounds that whilst it purports to show the superiority of the comprehensive schools, the schools which are covered in the survey are not representative of comprehensive schools in general. Thus only sixty-seven existent comprehensive schools are covered out of the 745 which had been established for more than seven years and which were largely uncreamed. Another criticism, again levelled at the survey, is that the schools surveyed were very unevenly spread throughout the country — only one school was surveyed in the Greater London area, although 15 per cent of national secondary school children attend Greater London schools. Forty-one of the schools were in county towns against only twenty-six in cities, suburbs and industrial conurbations. Once more the study is unable to offer any indication of the relative intake quality of these sixty-seven schools relative to that of the maintained system as a whole. The same criticisms of atypicality and uncertainty as to whether like is being compared with like dog this study also. In addition, Pedley's figures include pupils who achieved a CSE grade 1 as gaining an 'O' level equivalent. The official DES statistics for 1967/68 which yield a figure of 14.8 per cent of all school leavers gaining five or more 'O' level passes do not include CSE grade 1 passes. Once again it is best, therefore, that Pedley's results are treated with extreme caution.

In contrast to Pedley's claims that comprehensive schooling leads to higher rates of attainment than selective schooling, Davis (1967) argued that a consideration of the public examination results for 1965 in London schools shows the comprehensive schools to be performing no better than the secondary modern schools. Davis showed that the proportion of 'O' level candidates (as opposed to all pupils in the fifth year) who gained a pass was no higher in comprehensive schools than in secondary modern schools. This study is extraordinarily flawed, however, since Davis failed to consider whether entry rates in public examinations were simply more restrictive in London secondary modern schools than in London comprehensives (which was in fact the national trend). If this were the case the secondary modern schools may have achieved their equivalent pass rate merely by entering only their most able pupils for the 'O' level examination.

In 1970 Benn and Simon published the results of their survey of comprehensive schools carried out in 1968 in a volume entitled *Half Way There*. Unlike Pedley and Davis they made no attempt to carry out a direct comparison of the results of comprehensive schools and schools of other types. Instead, basing their survey on national statistics published by the DES, they sought to point out the relative performance of comprehensive schools in 1964 and 1967 compared with that of the grammar schools. Such an indirect comparison yielded the results that, whereas comprehensive schools were entering a dramatically higher number of candidates for 'O' level in 1967 than they were in 1964 (23,750 entrants compared with 13,130), the number of candidates entered by grammar schools fell by 8490. In all conscience, however, the figures and trends which Benn and Simon present mean nothing. Owing to the comprehensive reorganization taking place over these years in some area, the number of school leavers from comprehensive schools increased by 89 per cent in that period. It is hardly surprising, therefore, that Benn and Simon note a 'dramatic upward curve' in the number of pupils entering for examinations from comprehensive schools in this period. In fact the *proportion* of leavers who had taken 'O' level examinations changed very little in either type of school.

During the 1970s a number of studies appeared which compared the academic performance of the two systems of education in specific local areas either over time or at a specific point in time. These are briefly reviewed below:

1   In Oxfordshire, which went comprehensive in a piecemeal fashion between 1965 and 1974, the numbers of pupils entering 'A' level examinations increased and the pass rate as a proportion of entrants gaining 'A' level qualifications increased from 67 per cent in 1974 to 74 per cent in 1976 (Stevens, 1980).

2   Analyses of the public examination results for the Sheffield area in 1974 seemed to indicate that since comprehensivization examination pass rates had improved and during the years 1974 and 1979 the per pupil average for 'O' level/CSE equivalent passes obtained is said to have risen from 1.89 to 2.21 (Wright; 1977)

3   A comparison of the proportion of all leavers gaining one or more 'A' levels and five or more 'O' levels or CSE grade 1's in the 'selective school areas' of Aylesbury, Beaconsfield and High Wycombe with the 'comprehensive school area' of Milton Keynes (in Buckinghamshire) showed a much higher proportion of successful pupils in the selective school areas. However, when the intake quality of both systems was controlled the picture was reversed (Stevens, 1980).

4   The Welwyn area of Hertfordshire has recorded a 95 per cent rise in the number of 'O' levels gained and a 63 per cent rise in the number of 'A' level passes gained since comprehensivization (*ibid*).

5   A comparison of the pass rates of Leicestershire comprehensives with Leicester town selective schools for the years 1975/77 at 'O' level/ CSE grade 1 level and 'A' level showed the comprehensive schools to be performing better at all levels compared to the selective schools (Gaylon, 1979)

6   Research (quoted in Hopkins, 1979) carried out by Davies in a Midland county has shown that 15 per cent of all school leavers from comprehensive schools achieve one or more 'A' levels compared with 11 per cent of leavers in the selective sector. In this county, contrary

to the nationally prevailing pattern, selective schools had been retained in predominantly working class areas, giving this sector a poorer prognosis.

Sadly for our purposes each of these studies is flawed in similar ways to those of the major studies, and all local studies are compounded with local atypicality which it is difficult to control for or disentangle. Local complications aside, all but one of the studies offer no information about the relative intake quality of the different groups of pupils attending different types of school and this flaw is compounded in most of the studies by other flaws.

In 1975, 1977 and 1979, Raymond Baldwin, Chairman of the Governors of Manchester Grammar School and a contributor to the *Black Papers on Education*, offered the results of his own analyses of academic attainment rates in the two systems of education as proving that comprehensive schools inhibit academic attainment among their pupils. In 1975, in a publication entitled *The Great Comprehensive Gamble*, Baldwin analyzed national statistics of educational attainment at seven levels:

  (i)   those pupils gaining one CSE grade 4 pass or better;
  (ii) those pupils gaining five CSE grade 4 passes or better;
 (iii) those pupils gaining one or more 'O' level passes;
 (iv) those pupils gaining five or more 'O' level passes;
  (v) those pupils gaining at least one 'A' level pass;
 (vi) those pupils gaining three or more 'A' level passes;
(vii) those pupils awarded a university place.

He analyzed the data at these seven levels as indicating that whilst comprehensive schools were superior to the unreorganized sector at levels 1 and 2, the unreorganized sector does better at all other levels. Even at levels 1 and 2, Baldwin believes the comprehensive system's superiority to be a result merely of grammar school reluctance to enter pupils for CSE.

Baldwin's analysis compounds felony with felony. His first felony is the failure to take into account the fact that by 1974, the year to which his analysis refers, the selective system had become a 'rump', so whilst most secondary modern schools had been incorporated into the comprehensive system, a disproportionate number of grammar schools remained intact. Nationally, therefore, comprehensive schools were not getting their fair share of the most able children in the secondary school population — a fact confirmed by DES statistics, since in some thirty local authorities almost all of the top 15 per cent of the ability range attended a grammar school and in fifty-nine local authorities the top 8 per cent of the ability range attended grammar schools in 1967. A second felony is that Baldwin's analysis does not compare like with like. The analysis compares the examination results of areas which have been reorganized with those of unreorganized areas. As there still existed a trend in 1974 for the totally reorganised areas to be working class areas, rural areas or areas in Wales and since working class, rural and Welsh children tend to do less well in examinations, it is of little surprise that Baldwin's analysis presents the selective system as out-performing the comprehensive system.

In 1977, in *Black Paper 1977*, Baldwin published another analysis of comparative system performance based on DES figures for 1974/75. In an attempt to neutralize the effect of creaming on the comprehensive schools, he carried out a statistical adjustment, transferring 3 per cent of grammar school pupils to the comprehensive sector, crediting these pupils (7750 in 1974 and 6384 in 1975) with successes at the grammar school rate and similarly debiting the figures for the selective system. The results of this piece of wizardry led him to the conclusions that the switch to comprehensive education had not raised educational performance and that the rise in passes at CSE level was the result of the growth of the use of the examination and the raising of the school leaving age.

However, in both this study and his study of 'A' level results for 1976–77 released in 1979, which claimed to expose two alarming trends (that 'A' level results in the comprehensive sector have consistently lagged behind those in the selective sector and that the proportion of leavers gaining 'A' levels has declined since 1972), Baldwin considerably underestimates the real effect of creaming on the comprehensive system. In the case of his 1979 claim that the proportion of pupils gaining 'A' levels has dropped consistently since 1972, he has quite simply misread the statistics (see Venning, 1980).

One further study of examination results should be mentioned briefly: that carried out by Miles (1979) of the University of Hull into factors affecting pupil performance at 18+. The study analyzed the results of 6200 candidates for 'A' level and found very little relationship between the results gained and the type of school attended, once differences between the types of school in their intakes had been taken into account. Comprehensives' poor performance was simply explicable by intakes that were essentially of secondary modern calibre.

Studies using other measures of academic attainment

There are two further studies which fall into this category — one study by Lowenstein (1979) has yet to be fully published but his data suggested that whereas his sample of twenty children attending independent schools improved their IQ over five years, the reverse occurred in his sample of twenty attending comprehensive schools. Ford (1969) in her study of grammar, secondary modern and comprehensive schools in London, found no evidence to suggest that academic attainment rates in her streamed comprehensive schools were superior to those of the selective schools taken as a whole. Her comprehensive schools were, however, heavily creamed of top ability children.

All these studies of academic attainment levels at a point in time between different systems of education yield therefore little conclusive evidence. The vast majority of studies reviewed in the preceding pages are subject to deficiencies which prevent their ready acceptance. Perhaps the most common deficiency in these studies is the failure to ensure that judgments are made comparing like with like and the most common contributory factor to this failure is the inability of the studies to guarantee that when comparisons are made of academic 'output' from different systems they take into account the relative academic 'input' of pupils into the different school systems.

2   *Social Development — Truancy, Delinquency, Pupil Values and Attitudes, Social Mixing, Equality of Opportunity*

This section is divided into two. We will investigate firstly if there is a relationship between truancy and delinquency and the type of school attended by pupils. We will then review evidence relating to possible differences in values and attitudes, consciousness of class and social mixing in the comprehensive and the selective systems.

Truancy

Despite some estimates of increased London truancy rates (Rutter, 1980) in recent years and the extremely bleak picture painted by the editors of the *Black Papers*, it does seem that the answer to the question 'Has truancy increased as a result of comprehensive reorganization' is that we do not know. Reporting the results of his investigation into truancy in his book *Truancy*, Tyerman (1968) concludes that the indications are that there is an overall national attendance rate of around 90 per cent and that there is no sign of a general decline in attendance. He further concludes that whilst grammar schools tend to enjoy higher attendance rates than comprehensive schools, these schools in turn tend to have better attendance rates than secondary modern schools. According to Fogelman and Richardson (1974) truancy is strongly related to social class and rates are highest in the North of England and in Wales. Their study suggested there was little relationship between truancy and the type of school attended but found that within streamed schools truancy was disproportionately low in the higher streams and disproportionately high in the lower streams. A DES survey (quoted in Wright, 1977) of absenteeism on one day in January 1974 found, like Tyerman, 10 per cent of children in middle and secondary schools were absent with about 2 per cent of children absent without legitimate reason. All these studies present a remarkably consistent picture — a general absence rate in all British secondary schools of about 10 per cent and a truancy rate of about 2 per cent.

It would seem reasonable from the available evidence, deficient though it sometimes is, to conclude that there is a little evidence that truancy has marginally increased over the last decade and a half — a period covering the development of the comprehensive system — and that rates of truancy are most strongly related to social class and academic ability rather than to the type of school. Whether the temporal change reflects comprehensivization is unclear.

Delinquency

An evaluation of trends in delinquency is a similarly difficult task to carry out and in view of the absence of comparative studies of delinquency rates in different types of secondary school, an evaluation of the influence of comprehensive schooling on delinquency is almost impossible.

On the face of it, official delinquency (i.e., crimes detected by the police) has increased for both the 10–17 age group and the 17–21 age group over the last twenty years. In addition the crime rate of these two age groups appears to demonstrate a disproportionately high increase when compared with adult crime. Official statistics suggest a startling six-fold increase in the crime rate for 14–17 year old girls from a low base in 1957 and a three-fold increase for boys in the same age group (Rutter, 1980). Again, we must treat the statistics from which this trend is extrapolated with considerable caution. In interpreting crime rates, in general and juvenile crime rates in particular, we should be alert to the following: alterations in the law from time to time may alter what constitutes a crime and may have an effect on crime rates; the extent and pattern of policy activity will influence what sort of people and what number of people are convicted; and crime levels are influenced by the situations and the opportunities that are available for committing crime (*ibid*).

Delinquency amongst adolescents, then, appears to have increased over the last twenty years. It appears to be strongly correlated with low social class position (see the review in West, 1982) but there is an absence of any evidence which might suggest a relationship between delinquency and comprehensivisation.

Other social outcomes

A small number of studies in the last twenty years have (i) looked at the difference in pupil attitudes and values in selective and comprehensive systems; (ii) compared the extent to which pupils in both types of system are conscious of their own social class position and its implications for their future life opportunities; and (iii) attempted to assess whether there is a higher level of social mixing between classes in the comprehensive system than in the selective system. In addition there is a small body of work which attempts to assess the extent to which educational opportunity has been made more equal in the comprehensive schools of England and Wales. This work is now considered.

Values, Attitudes and Consciousness of Class

In 1961 Miller published a comparative study of the values of four groups of 13–14 year old boys in comprehensive, grammar and modern schools: boys who attended a grammar school; boys who attended a comprehensive school but were of 'grammar school ability'; boys who attended a comprehensive school and were of secondary modern school ability; and boys who attended a secondary modern school. The findings of his study suggested a closer agreement between the boys in the comprehensive schools in their positive appreciation of their schools than was found in pupils in the selective system. Miller also found that the extra curricular interests of boys in the 'comprehensive-modern' group were 'culturally superior' to those of their counterparts in the secondary modern school, whilst the interests of the 'comprehensive/grammar' pupils showed inferiority to those of grammar school pupils. Thirdly, Miller found that there were similarly few indications of anti-school attitudes in the comprehensive and grammar schools, whilst an anti-school culture was more evident in the secondary modern schools. Finally, Miller could find no clear indication that comprehensive schools promoted greater social integration of children of different social classes than selective schools. Miller himself attaches significant caveats to these findings. He is of the opinion that the difficulties he encountered in matching schools from the two systems in terms of curricular and extra curricular facilities make it difficult to posit with certainty a causal relationship between pupil experience of comprehensive schooling and his findings. He also speculates that any differences in values and attitudes among pupils in the two systems may reflect the effect of the power of the comprehensive school as an innovation (as it was in the late 1950s) in generating higher morale than the established selective schools.

Social Mixing

Ford (1969), in her much quoted book, reported that interaction between children of different social class origins was no greater and was probably less in the streamed comprehensive schools she studied than in her grammar schools. The same study also claims to demonstrate that comprehensive school pupils are as likely to promote perceptions of a rigid and dichotomous class structure as selective schools. The validity of these findings and of other findings from this study quoted elsewhere in this chapter has been questioned by critics who argue that the London comprehensive schools of her study can hardly be regarded as typical of all British comprehensive schools as they were highly creamed socially and academically.

Equality of Opportunity

Finally in this section we consider the evidence of research which has attempted to investigate whether comprehensive schools generate greater equality of educational opportunity for children of equal talent, irrespective of their social class position.

Dixon (1962), Holly (1963) and Ford (1969) all conclude that in the streamed comprehensive schools which they studied there is strong evidence that children with high social class are more likely to be allocated to academic streams. Holly and Ford find this initial advantage to be sustained or exaggerated throughout pupils' school life. On the other hand, Dixon finds less premature leaving among pupils in lower streams and a more liberal examination entry policy in his comprehensive schools than in his selective schools. Also, Eggleston (1967), in a study of comprehensive schools in eight Midland counties, found that the comprehensive schools' rate of retention for pupils of all social classes was significantly higher than the rate of selective schools in the same counties. In all of the studies the comprehensive schools investigated had retained streaming.

In summary, then, the effect of the comprehensive system on the social development of its pupils is once more less than clear. Levels of truancy, as measured by failure to register at school without a legitimate reason, appear to be most strongly related to social class position and academic ability and appear to show minimal change over time, although, of course, post-registration truancy may be strategically easier in large comprehensive schools than in small schools of any type. Delinquency levels, which again show a strong relationship to social class position, appear to have increased drastically over the last twenty years but there is an absence of evidence which might demonstrate any relationship between rates of delinquency and types of school. Attitudes to school and pupil values appear, according to some small-scale studies, to be affected positively by pupil experience of comprehensive education, although there are serious doubts raised by some of the researchers themselves about whether such differences demonstrate the effect of comprehensive education per se. There is little available evidence to suggest that higher levels of social mixing are fostered by comprehensive schools, though studies which examine this often investigate comprehensive schools creamed of high social class, academic pupils. Finally, there seems to be little evidence that comprehensive schools equalize educational opportunity for children of equal talent irrespective of their social class position. But again in three of the four studies cited, the comprehensive schools studied were streamed from intake and therefore the studies can tell us little about the possible effect of non-selective comprehensive schools. The research studies can in fact tell us surprisingly little about the social effects of comprehensive schooling and the realization of such lack of knowledge should be a salutary jolt to us twenty years after government support for comprehensive education and some thirty or more years since the establishment of the first comprehensive schools.

The Recent Work on the Effects of Comprehensive School Organization

In addition to the studies already reviewed, there has recently been a further flurry of studies that compare the school systems.

Perhaps the most scientific attempt to assess the effects of the comprehensive system lies in the data collected by the National Children's Bureau (NCB) in its long-term cohort study of the progress of 16,000 young people born in one week of 1958 (Steedman, 1980). At different ages the children were tested and schools were questioned, thus providing a wide range of information on heath, economic factors, housing and educational outcomes. Information was specifically obtained on the characteristics of the sample at age 11 on entry to the different types of school — grammars, secondary moderns and comprehensives — and information was further obtained on a wide range of academic and social outcomes at age 16 as the sample left school. After controlling statistically for variations in the ability and social composition of the intakes into the different systems of education (the comprehensives actually had intakes little different from those of the secondary modern schools as the former were heavily creamed), there seemed to be little difference in the results of the selective and comprehensive systems. In terms of mathematics and reading comprehension, the lower ability children seemed to progress at a similar pace in the two systems, though the very low ability child may have been slightly better off in the comprehensives. The very able child also seemed unaffected — or affected equally — by the two systems. Although there were hints of increased social class mobility in the comprehensives, on some of the social or affective outcomes, comprehensives underperformed the selective system — truancy rates were higher, teachers perceived a higher proportion of pupils as having disturbance of personality or behaviour and the parents of comprehensive school pupils tended to be less satisfied with their children's schools. On the other more academic outcomes of a pupil desire to stay on and pupil attitudes to later study, the comprehensives did slightly better than the selective system. Overall, though, comprehensives did as well as the selectives.

The information on the public examination attainments of the sample at 16 (Steedman, 1983) was published some two years after the above findings and presents a very similar picture of minimal differences between the two systems. When grammar and secondary modern school pupils were treated as a selective system, once differences in intake had been controlled for there was no difference in the proportions gaining no examination passes; in the average number of 'O' level/equivalents or the proportion getting five or more passes; in the proportion attaining an 'O' level/equivalent pass in maths and English; in the average number of 'A' levels obtained and in the grades obtained. Whilst there were slight differences between the three types of comprehensives described in the study (the 'transitional' comprehensives did particularly badly whilst the 'early' and 'recent' schools did better), overall the National Children's Bureau summarized its findings as showing that '. . . after correcting for differences in initial attainment and background before secondary school, comprehensive pupils at this time (1974) were neither failing to match nor surpassing the examination performance of the selective pupils' (Fogelman and Holden, 1983, p. 9).

Another recent attempt to assess the effectiveness of comprehensive reorganization was provided by analysis of data at the Scottish Education Data Archive, collected through a series of national surveys of Scottish school leavers (Gray, McPherson and Raffe, 1983). There are, of course, substantial differences in the history, past mode of functioning and present organization of the Scottish education system by comparison with England and Wales — one study for example, which shows Scottish children moving from above average reading ability at 7 to below average attainment at 16 (Fogelman, 1983). Tibbenham (1978) cautions that 'the outstanding feature to emerge is the difference between the situation in Scottish comprehensives and that in the rest of Britain'. It is also important to remember as the authors themselves note that their data cover the early years of comprehensive reorganization and define as comprehensive only the sixty-nine 'common' schools which were completely uncreamed by the selective system or by any 'rogue' remaining super-selective schools. These schools seem to have been situated in socially unusual areas, which may explain their apparent success.

These researchers' results are generally more favourable to the comprehensive system than are most of the earlier studies. In the affective areas of truancy, satisfaction with school and levels of corporal punishment (included as a surrogate measure for behaviour), there were no appreciable differences between systems. Academic attainment levels were slightly higher in comprehensives — fewer pupils left with no qualifications and rather more left with three or more 'higher' passes. Class inequality in attainment was also slightly reduced in the comprehensives but this seems again to be in part a reflection of the historical tradition of the areas where the unusual uncreamed comprehensives were situated.

There are seven other recent studies of the effects of comprehensive education which cover academic outcomes only. The first study is on the city of Salisbury (Naylor, 1983) and concentrates on a comparison of examination results in the one-third of the city that has gone comprehensive with those in the two-thirds of the city that has retained the selective system. Using the examination results of the first cohort of pupils to go through the two systems and with no attempt to control for variation in the social and academic quality of intakes into the two systems, the author proclaims the selective schools' superiority with evidence that the number of higher grades per pupil was 3.1 in the selective system and only 1.6 in the comprehensive system and that in some subjects — Physics and French particularly — the advantage of the selective system is three-fold or greater. The absence of any intake data, the evidence that the selective sector is still creaming the comprehensive system and the evidence that the selective system is creaming high ability pupils even from outside the city make the author's interpretations highly suspect.

The second study (Davis, 1984) looked at historical trends in one city — Leicester — and found that although the proportion of pupils gaining at least one 'O' level or CSE equivalent has risen from 36 per cent (when the city was selective in 1976) to 37.5 per cent in 1981 (after comprehensive reorganization), the proportion of pupils actually getting six or more 'O' levels or CSE equivalents dropped from 12 per cent to 9 per cent. Although the author claims that this 'spreading' of success over a wider ability range is the result of comprehensive reorganization, the extent to which simple temporal change is at work is unclear. Since the proportion of pupils attaining one or more 'O' levels or equivalents in the city has actually increased by less than the national average between 1976 and 1981, it is possible to infer from this data which for the full ability range as well as for 'high fliers' success rates, comprehensives do not do particularly well.

The third series of studies has been published by the National Council for Education Standards (Cox and Marks 1983, 1985 and 1986). The 1983 study shows variation in examination results between LEAs of similar social class composition (a factor of up to two) and between some schools within LEAs (a factor of up to four). They also find that the selective system obtains better results than comprehensives (30–40 per cent more 'O' level examination passes per pupil). Using a data base of the 1981 examination results and census data on a number of social variables, the authors used data from fifty-four out of ninety-six English LEAs in an attempt to support their belief that a return to selective education would improve examination attainments.

In the report's favour it has a large data base, recent data and also explicitly attempts to control for the effect of background environmental factors on the two systems' relative performances. There are, however, major flaws in the methodology of the study. Firstly, the LEAs the study uses are unrepresentative in that they contain all selective LEAs but less than one-third of fully comprehensive ones. Secondly, only one background variable is used to attempt to statistically 'neutralize' the effects generated by the comprehensive LEAs' more disadvantaged socioeconomic structure — the variable of the proportion of the population in low social classes — yet we have other recent evidence (DES, 1983; Gray, Jesson and Jones, 1984) that additional variables would have added considerably to the proportion of variance in examination performance explained. Adding the variable ethnicity to a social class variable increased the amount of variance explained in staying on at school rates by 10 per cent, whilst other variables on housing conditions, unemployment, free school meal rates etc. added about 3 per cent more (DES, 1983). In the Gray, Jesson and Jones (1984) study, the proportion of children living in low social class households explains 58.1 per cent of the variation in the proportion of children attaining more than one 'O' level pass across ninety-six LEAs — adding other variables on the proportion in high social classes, children with parents born abroad and children living in one parent families increased this figure to 73.7 per cent. Clearly, much of the apparent superiority of the selective system could be due to the study's intake variables explaining little variation in outcome and therefore explaining as due to school effects variation that is due to outside-school social and evironmental factors (for further criticisms see Gray and Jones, 1983).

There are, of course, numerous other criticisms of the study. LEAs are allocated to a social class 'group' of LEAs for analysis, but, of course, within each LEA there are high and low class areas. The social class variable 'proportion of population in high social class' is not utilized, yet DES statisticians assert (DES, 1984a) in their critique of the report 'that the real correlation is between high SEG and good examination results rather than low SEG and bad examination results'. Perhaps the most cogent set of criticisms (together with an analysis using a different but more representative data base) appears in Gray, Jesson and Jones (1984), who conclude their own analysis of LEA examination and catchment area data by arguing that '. . . knowing whether an LEA had organised its schools on a fully comprehensive basis or had retained selection to some extent did not make a difference to its overall level of examination results'. Their own results show that, as expected, '. . . the more adequately we controlled for differences in social composition between LEA's, the more the importance of the form of school organisation was diminished' (p. 55). Those authorities with fully comprehensive systems of school organization produced, in this research, examination results which were in all respects comparable to those organized on a selective basis.

The second Cox and Marks' study (1985) repeated many of the points of the earlier work. Using fifty-seven LEAs, the 1982 examination results and other sources of data, the authors again argue that pupils at secondary modern and grammar schools together obtained more 'O' level passes than those at comprehensives — between 30–40 per cent more per pupil when looked at nationally. When LEAs of similar social class grouping are compared on the basis of their comprehensiveness and 'selectivity', differences still favour the selective LEAs. Grammar schools overall do consistently well — more surprisingly, secondary modern schools do very well with results only marginally inferior to the comprehensives and with particularly good results in Maths and English.

Many of the same criticisms that were levelled at the first study were applied, some with reduced applicability, to the second study (Gray, Jesson and Jones, 1985). There are, again, doubts as to whether the more socially disadvantaged LEAs which have comprehensive systems have had this disadvantage taken account of, even though Cox and Marks added a measure on high social class to add to the measure on low social class. If one takes *all* 'O' and CSE grades to measure the effectiveness of the two systems, then the percentage of pupils in grammar school in an LEA (what is called the selectivity variable) makes no difference at all to the examination results obtained by Gray and his colleagues.

The third study from the National Council for Educational Standards (Cox and Marks, 1986) concentrates upon the schools and the results of the Inner London Education Authority. Their argument here concentrates on a comparison of the fully comprehensive ILEA system with selective systems elsewhere, a comparison which is alleged to show substaintial ILEA under-performance. Critics have noted however that the study took as its baseline examination statistics for 1981 and 1982, yet the 1981 cohort were the last intake into the old system of heavily creamed comprehensives. Doubt is also cast on the studies allowance for the high level of social disadvantage in London, a doubt which has been confirmed by the more elaborate statistical procedures used elsewhere (DES, 1984b) which have revealed ILEA schools to be performing precisely at the levels one would predict from knowledge of the area's socio-economic structure.

The last two studies we consider here are those of Maughan and Rutter (1986) and the further findings of the reanalyzed DES study (1984b). Unfortunately for believers in the value of the comprehensive experiment, both these studies by independent researchers (which are in many ways some of the most scientific attempts yet to gain information on this question), have generated results unfavourable to comprehensive schooling. The Rutter study for example (Maughan and Ruter, 1987) draws upon data from the sample of children who furnished data for the *Fifteen Thousand Hours* study of school differences (Rutter *et al*, 1979). Taking similar children going into the two different systems and statistically controlling for the effects of any differences in intake into the systems, reading scores at age 14 were significantly higher in the selective grammar school sample by comparison with those children at comprehensive schools. Fifth year examination results — expressed in terms of 'points' scored for both CSE and 'O' levels — were also superior in the selective system, part of this being due to a higher entry rate in the grammar schools. When account was taken of this, though, by looking at the examination 'points' per entry, the selective system's superiority was reduced. Differences in sixth form examination results also favoured the selective schools but again these differences were reduced (but not eliminated) after allowing for the selective schools' higher entry rates.

The authors conclude their analysis with two points. They note that the selective schools' overperformance seems largely to be a function of their intellectual balance, whereby pupils seem to evoke high performance from each other. Comprehensive schools with an intake of similar ability to the grammar schools have only slightly lower examination attainments. Also, the authors note that *some* comprehensive schools can match the performance of the selective grammar schools. One school, with a relatively poor balance in its intake, succeeded because of its positive and cohesive ethos in bringing the attainments of both able and less able children up to their maximum. Overall, though, the authors results can only be seen as reflecting relatively unfavourably upon the academic outcomes of comprehensive schooling in inner London in the late 1970s.

The last study that we consider here is that conducted by the Statistics Branch of the Department of Education and Science (DES, 1984b). Based on ninety-six English LEAs, the analysis attempts to use socio-economic data on each LEA to explain variation in their educational outcomes in examination attainments. Socio-economic variables are very strongly associated with educational performance — for lower levels of examination attainment the social disadvantage factors were the most important influence in the amount of variation explained, whilst for higher levels of attainment the proportion of an LEA population in high socio-economic groups came into prominence. Several of the school-based variables were found to have statistically significant associations with the attainment measures but of a small degree. These variables included teacher turnover, pupil/teacher ratio and expenditure per head on education. Also — and most importantly for us here — the proportion of pupils in grammar schools in an LEA was associated with high 'A' level and 'O' level/CSE performance and was also associated with a low proportion of pupils leaving school with no graded result. Again, in this data set also, comprehensive schools appear to slightly underperform academically compared to the selective system.

Conclusions

In spite of the number of studies we have reviewed here, what seems most surprising is the relative paucity of the overall effort that has gone into research on this question. By comparison with research into topics such as classroom behaviour, school effectiveness or pupil/teacher interaction, Derrick (1980, p. 342) notes aptly that 'The evidence of widespread and increasing indifference or inability of researchers or of research funding agencies to pursue the comprehensive/selective topic is surprising ...'. Whilst the sheer difficulty of research in this area, the possible commitment of researchers to the comprehensive system and the difficulty of gaining research access may be contributory factors, the full explanation for this state of ignorance is unclear.

Overall, the research can tell us very little about the effectiveness of comprehensive schools. Looking first at academic attainment, comparisons of reading and arithmetical standards over time are difficult to relate to comprehensivization, given the myriad of other social factors that may also have generated these changes. Expansion in the proportion of pupils getting 'O' levels and CSEs may, as Heath (1984, p. 123) notes, 'have taken place *in* comprehensive schools but we cannot conclude that they happened *because* of comprehensive reorganisation'. Comparisons of the two system's academic performance at a point in time seem singularly equivocal — those studies showing a selective system advantage seem to be comparing that system with heavily creamed comprehensives. On social development, whether the slight rise in official truancy or the rise in delinquency is due to comprehensivization is again impossible to say. Studies on social attitudes, social mixing and equality of opportunity seem, on balance, to show minimal differences between the two systems.

Whilst most of the early work in this area was fatally flawed by the tendency of researchers to compare a full ability range selective system with a restricted ability range comprehensive system, recent research has been able to take account of these problems of comparison by statistical adjustment of system outcomes to reflect the differences in systems' intake quality. Disregarding the NCES study because of flawed methodology, the NCDS cohort suggests comprehensives to be academically similar but socially marginally inferior in their outcomes by comparison with the selective system, a trend confirmed by the Scottish data's suggestions of better comprehensive academic performance and only equivalent social outcomes. Set against this are the DES and Rutter findings of inferior comprehensive academic performance.

Overall though, it is the *lack* of effect that comprehensives have had on pupil development that appears so impressive. Whilst this may reflect the lack of difference between the comprehensives and the selective system in ethos, curriculum and internal organization, the failure of the schools to move towards the attainment of their goals seems to us to be marked and to be depressing.

Aside from studies using comprehensives with a full ability range, what is clearly also missing from the research enterprise is any evaluation of *why* comprehensive schools have generally failed to out-perform the selective system, since none of the studies reviewed has any data on the within school processes of the comprehensives that must logically be implicated. We have indications from early sociological case studies that the schools may be somewhat bilateral in their organization, recreating under one roof the divisions of the selective system (Benn and Simon, 1970). There are suggestions even that unstreaming may generate within mixed ability groups the same social class inequalities in attainment that existed between classes in a streamed setting (Ball, 1981). The pupil sub-cultures of the comprehensives appear in a recent account (Turner, 1983) very like those reported from the selective system (Woods, 1979; Lacey, 1970). Comprehensives appear to have 'Newsom' departments for the lower ability pupils, where various truces and negotiations are managed (Burgess, 1983) that bear an uncanny resemblance to day-to-day life in our own secondary modern school sample (Reynolds, 1975).

In the Burgess study in fact, the Newsom department for 'ROSLA children' was a kind of non-academic operation for low ability children that was in no sense in accordance with comprehensive principles of equality of educational opportunity.

Other work has focussed on the processes of pupil transfer from junior to senior school (Measor and Woods, 1984), on the implications of mixed ability teaching for teachers and for pupils (Evans, 1985; Corbishley *et al*, 1981), on control problems in classrooms and in the schools (Denscombe, 1984), on the comprehensive sixth form (Buswell, 1984), on teacher careers and life passages in the schools (Sykes, Measor and Woods, 1985) and on pupil/teacher interaction (Beynon, 1985; Hammersley and Woods, 1985).

We also have three further sets of literature on comprehensive schools. One set has used the 'site' of a comprehensive school or of comprehensive schools to generate ideas of more theoretical relevance to the sociology of education. Work on coping strategies (Hargreaves, 1978), teacher ideology (Hargreaves, A, 1982; Hammersley, 1982) and comprehensive schools' relationship to ongoing political struggles (Hunter, 1983 and 1984; Simon 1986) falls into this category.

The second set of material has been generated by those with very committed, often polemical, views on the future of the comprehensive school. These are by academics like Sayer (1985) and Hargreaves D, (1982), as well as by practitioners like Boyson (1974), Dawson (1981) and Barker (1986).

The third set of material has been the large volume of research conducted in the organization and management tradition at the National Foundation for Educational Research. There were some early studies of comprehensive schooling (Monks, 1968 and 1970) but these are heavily dated, were of heavily creamed schools and of course had no selective system comparison built in. The information on within school-processes was also rudimentary. Later studies have generated valuable information on such areas of the schools as mixed ability teaching (Reid *et al*, 1983) and the impact of falling rolls upon staff provision (Walsh *et al*, 1984).

Overall though, the research that we have on comprehensive schooling is still pitifully small when one considers the magnitude of the educational change that they represent. Work on the secondary modern school (Woods, 1979; Turner, 1969; Partridge, 1966) is smaller still in quantity, whilst that on the grammar school (Davis, 1967; King, 1969) is rudimentary. There *is* work on the comprehensive schools, as described in our last few pages, but this has been done on the comprehensives because they are schools rather than specifically on the schools because they are comprehensives. In all the above material, no selective school comparisons are built in and so we are unable to discuss whether the internal processes of the schools, their ethos, their organisation and their pupil outcomes are because they are simply secondary schools or because they are comprehensive schools.

All in all, the absence of comparative work comparing full ability range comprehensives with the selective system and the absense of work on the comparative processes of the two systems paints a depressing picture. This study is aimed at remedying the situation.

Part Two: The Local Study

Chapter 3

Treliw, its Educational System and
Our Research Design

The only direct way to understand the process by which learning is affected by the school environment is to undertake detailed longitudinal studies comparing children with similar measured abilities early in their school careers who are subsequently exposed to contrasting school experiences.   (Sarane Boocock)

The community we undertook our research in has been described by us at length elsewhere (Reynolds *et al*, 1987), although a few important points bear repetition. The history of Treliw is closely dependent upon the history of its past major employer — the coal industry. The growth in the industry made the community a boom town — people were sucked into what was a crucible of a community from other areas of Wales and from the West Country.

The community itself had — and to an extent still has — distinctive characteristics. It was a close knit population, where people related to others both because of geographical proximity in the terraced streets but also because the dangers, deprivations and disasters of life encouraged people to help each other. Education was held in high esteem and the community concentrated upon the provision of high levels of grammar school places.

Religion, because of rural migration, was important and much social life centred on the chapel. Politics, too, became a concern of the Treliw population and the community played a founding role in the formation of the Labour party, a political commitment that was solidified by the strikes, lock outs and class conflict endemic in South Wales in the 1920s and 1930s. Culturally too the area was alive with choirs, brass bands, operatic societies, drama groups and other societies. It was, like the community of Hoggart (1973), a traditional collectivistic, conservative, working class society.

Many forces have subsequently combined to erode the distinctiveness, the collectivism, the cohesion and the control over individual consciousness exercised by that community. Television has broadened horizons and the migration of probably the most able has taken from the community many who would have been prominent in its artistic, musical and cultural life.

Industry is now more differentiated and people from the community work in many different settings — if they do work that is. Changing housing conditions have led to a growth in 'home centredness', with people now being more content to spend time indoors with their family rather than interacting with the community. The building of council estates also has eroded many old communities and destroyed extended family links — old people are segregated into separate grouped flats and young families are placed in the estates, where status has to be achieved rather than being ascribed. Unemployment has, according to many local respondents, sapped morale and made people lose hope. What people need, we were continually told, is a renewed sense of faith in the future, yet the community itself is no longer the organized group that seems able to fight for one.

The community now is certainly similar to many other areas in the Midlands, the North, London and Central Scotland in its high levels of economic deprivation. In 1985, as our studies came to an end, its death rate was 14.7 per thousand, compared to 11.7 for England and Wales. Only 80.1 per cent of houses had exclusive use of all amenities, compared to 95.3 per cent in England and Wales. Only 9.4 per cent of the employed population was in social classes 1 and 2 — 17.2 per cent were so in England and Wales. Semi-skilled and unskilled workers comprised 34.3 per cent of all workers in Treliw and 22 per cent in England and a Wales. Its male unemployment rate was above 25 per cent, compared to Welsh rate of 16 per cent and a British rate of 13 per cent at the time of writing.

In spite of the economic changes and the problems that they have brought, there is much impressionistic evidence that the community life of the area, if weaker, is still a force for the social control of its inhabitants in ways that do not exist in more anomic, differentiated and fragmented communities such as the inner city areas. Many families are still of the extended type and exhibit that mixing of young and old that ensures a continuity of respectable values. Rates of adult crime are the same as the British average. The proportion of single parent households is 14.2 per cent (the same as the British figure) and is kept low by informal sanctions against marriage break up and still existing traditions that boys should marry girls that get accidentally pregnant. Dress is conformist, even amongst the young. Social mores as to codes of social, sexual and moral conduct are conventional and strongly enforced by the informal social systems of the community. Whilst the economic base of the area has been destroyed, the community base has merely been damaged by the social changes of the last two decades.

Young people growing up in Treliw are likely to be from homes and communities exhibiting what control theorists (Hargreaves, 1981; Hirschi, 1969) would argue is high levels of control, where they are socialized into pro-social rather than anti-social conduct and values by the attachments they form within and without the family. Whilst the economic problems of the community in the 1970s made the comprehensive experiment a difficult one, since economic factors and unemployment could be expected to affect pupils' attitudes to school work, the control exercised by the community would have gone some considerable way towards giving the experiment a good chance of success. Treliw exhibits poverty, not pathology, whereas many deprived communities would have exhibited both and made the new schools task more difficult.

Education in Wales and in Treliw

Before going on to consider the comprehensive experiment and our assessment of it in detail, it is important to be aware of the nature of the Welsh education system as the context within which Treliw is situated. It is clear historically that the Welsh have as one of our respondents told us 'worshipped at the shrine of education' for over a century. Perhaps because of the status given to the learned person by Welsh language culture, perhaps because of the instrumentality of Welsh non-conformity, perhaps because of the general economic insecurity of the nation and perhaps because of the commitment of the Labour party to ensure a chance for the Welsh to be upwardly mobile, enthusiasm for education in Wales has been marked. Gittins (1967) noted the existence of parental attitudes to education more favourable than parental social class would predict and historical accounts (Rees, 1980) note the desire of Welsh miners to educate their sons to avoid the prospects of pit employment, in contrast to Yorkshire where sons following their fathers into the mines was more accepted. Whilst Raymond Williams' oft quoted assertions in his *Politics and Letters* that '. . . there was absolutely no sense in which education was felt to be something curious in the community . . . there was nothing wrong with being bright, winning a scholarship or writing a book' may reflect a degree of selective perception, there is no doubt his views are widely shared in Wales.

Wales historically has therefore been a high spender on education, with per pupil expenditure at secondary level for its eight LEAs usually some 5–6 per cent ahead of the English mean for its 96 LEAs (Reynolds, 1983). Byrne and Williamson (1975) note in their discussion of Merthyr Tydfil the very generous expenditure on teachers' salaries in particular, and the high expenditure levels overall, higher than one would have expected from authorities of similar social class composition elsewhere. Much of this excess expenditure, however, went upon the education of the able in grammar schools, which the Welsh LEAs consistently overprovided relative to England — in the 1960s in those Welsh LEAs not already comprehensive (mostly in urban South Wales), grammar school education was provided for over 30 per cent of all pupils, rising to 40 per cent in some communities. This compares with an English rate of approximately 20 per cent going to grammar school (as in the Douglas cohort) in the 1960s.

There is no doubt these schools had high status in their communities — many of them have actually been lionized in accounts written by former teachers or headteachers (for example, of Cowbridge Grammar by Iolo Davies, 1967). Getting a child to grammar school was widely seen as a major goal for parents — in our first study in the Treliw secondary moderns, the very high figure of 70.9 per cent of the mothers of our sample would have wanted their child to go to grammar school. Teaching to the tests used for the 11+ consequently became a major task in many of the Welsh primary schools. The grammar schools had a higher proportion of graduate teachers (and not a few with doctorates), higher per capita expenditure, smaller class sizes and generally a more conducive educational environment than the other schools.

By contrast, the Welsh secondary modern schools were of low status, low resources, few graduate teachers and lower per capita expenditure. To be allocated to them at eleven was widely taken by pupils and parents to be failure. Because of the high provision of grammar school places, very few potential sixth-form pupils would have gone to the schools — assuming 30 per cent creaming by the grammars, virtually all children with IQs of above 115 would have been outside the schools. 'O' level or CSE examination classes in years four and five would likewise have been drained of a large number of their potential examination candidates, a situation completely different to that of England where many secondary modern schools were able to enter a large proportion of their older pupils for examinations and even to develop sixth forms aiming at 'A' levels. Not surprisingly, curriculum development was minimal. Likewise, whereas English authorities embarked on a major programme of new building of secondary modern schools to cope with the bulge in the size of the secondary age cohort, these factors were of less importance in parts of Wales where population was declining. Welsh secondary moderns were, therefore, in old and inadequate buildings.

The effect of these sharply differentiated traditions of academic training for all who could benefit in the grammar schools and a more vocational, less academic experience in the secondary moderns was to create high levels of success for some and also high levels of failure for others. In the early 1970s, Byrne and Williamson (1975) reported very high rates of pupils staying on at school in their Merthyr sample and Wales comfortably exceeded England in the proportion of pupils attaining five or more 'O' levels, the proportion gaining two or more 'A' levels, the proportion staying on at school and the proportion of pupils going on to higher education. On the other hand, the system generated a much higher proportion of pupils with no academic qualifications whatsoever — whereas the English system got this 'failure' rate down to 15 per cent by the mid-1970s, the Welsh rate stayed in the region of 25–28 per cent in those same years (Reynolds, 1982a) although there has been a recent improvement (Reynolds and Murgatroyd, 1985).

What evidence we have on the operation of the internal processes of the Welsh comprehensive system as it emerged by the late 1970s suggests a traditional orientation and organisation, aiming at the development of the talents of the able as its primary goal. The sixth-forms have been argued to be more closed than elsewhere, with the existence of blocks on the development of the new sixth (NUT, 1975). The system exhibits higher levels of physical punishment than England (Society of Teachers Opposed to Physical Punishment, 1983). Streaming is argued to have been retained in a substantial number of schools (Loosemore, 1981) and in fact Inspectorate publications in Wales have been notably more cautious about unstreaming or mixed ability teaching than those in England. Curricular innovations such as the development of CSE. Mode 3 courses to make the curriculum more relevant, meaningful and teachable for the lower ability child have been underdeveloped in comparison with England — only 12 per cent of Welsh subject entries use Mode 3, compared to 22 per cent for the Associated Examination Board in England for example (*ibid*). Whether this reflects lack of school enthusiasm or restrictive policies by the Welsh examination board (the Welsh Joint Examination Committee) is unclear, although recent evidence suggests the problem is school based (Reynolds, 1983). Examination entry policy in Wales also is more restrictive than in England — of the 21 per cent of children who attained no qualifications when leaving in 1980/81, 19.1 per cent had not been entered for any examinations whatsoever. Impressionistic evidence suggests Welsh schools entering for English and mathematics only down to the bottom 15 per cent of the ability range, whilst in England policy in many schools is to enter right down into the remedial streams for such core subjects (Reynolds, 1982a).

Whereas rural Wales went comprehensive extremely rapidly in the 1960s and early 1970s for both ideological reasons concerned with equality of opportunity and because population decline was reducing the size of some of the grammar and modern schools to levels where broad curricular provision could not be guaranteed, South Wales was in general slower to move, with the exception of the capital city of Cardiff. Some have explained this as due to the inadequacy of most of the sets of school buildings for comprehensive organization — many were very old, lacking the space to provide the extra facilities, science laboratories and language laboratories that would be necessary to open up academic educational opportunities to the former secondary modern school children. Many have argued that Welsh authorities pragmatically held back the submission of schemes to ensure that central government gave the necessary sanction for new school building (Byrne and Williamson, 1975). Alternatively, it also seems likely that among some authorities the grammar school was held in high esteem as the avenue of social mobility for working class boys and girls, which produced a desire to ensure that the new comprehensives be launched effectively, with planning and foresight so as not to threaten the high academic standards formerly obtained. It is also possible — and we have heard it alleged — that many local politicians, pressured by the more activist parents of grammar school pupils, actually did not want to see the grammar schools destroyed, even if the comprehensives were to be grammar schools for all. A radical Socialist orientation to the wider social world could therefore co-exist with an educational philosophy which owed much to the elitism of Plato within parts of South Wales.

In some ways, the educational experience of Wales is therefore different from that of England. Even English areas having similar social class composition were unlikely to provide the same proportion of grammar school places or to have had the same enthusiasm for education. The success of the able, the failure of the less able and the two separate traditions of education for these groups of children is something distinctive.

The absence of change in the system over the last fifteen years is also marked, although there are those who think that this is potentially to Wales' advantage (Reynolds, 1983) since Wales can now learn productively from England's mistakes.

The net effect of all these factors has been to create in Wales what must be called a relatively ineffective secondary school sector. Rates of non-attendance in Wales are considerably higher than in England according to the 1974 DES survey of absenteeism — whereas in England 9.6 per cent of pupils were absent in a given day, Wales recorded figures of 13.9 per cent, a substantial gap later confirmed by analysis of regional data from the National Children's Bureau's 1958 cohort (Fogelman, 1983). Concern about examination attainment in Wales has been widespread from the late 1970s and the important Mold Conference (Welsh Office, 1978) up until the more recent debate (Reynolds and Murgatroyd, 1981 and 1983). Assessment of Performance Unit data give major grounds for concern about the secondary system's effectiveness — on mathematics, Welsh children achieve the highest scores of all British regions at age 11 (even including attainment on 'new' mathematics) yet are bottom of all regions by age 15 (Assessment of Performance Unit, 1982a and 1982b). On reading and writing ability, Wales moves from a similar mean score to England at age 11 to a lower score at 15. On science — a subject that can be argued to be virtually completely school dependent — Wales is top of all British regions on all sub-scales at 11, and bottom of all regions on all sub-scales at 15, sometimes by a large margin (Assessment of Performance Unit, 1982c, 1982d, 1982e and 1983).

Whilst inadequate buildings may be to blame for some of these problems, it seems likely that Wales simply has a less effective system of secondary schooling than elsewhere. Whilst the evidence from the emerging school effectiveness literature (Rutter, 1983; Reynolds, 1985a and 1985b; Reynolds *et al*, 1987) is that the effective school seems to be well managed, to be 'canny' about the need to ensure commitment is being won from its pupils and to be motivating as many pupils as possible through involving them the picture that is emerging of this effective school — particularly on academic effectiveness where the evidence is most clear — suggests that such institutions may well be more prevalent in England than in Wales. High levels of parental involvement, of visiting the schools and of involvement in educational matters are high attainment generating — Wales scores lower than England on this factor. A move to unstreaming or banding of some kind has been found in our own South Wales research to be associated with more favourable outcomes — again, Wales probably scores lower than England on this. On many other indicators also, Wales may well (if impressionistic evidence is correct) have less effective schools — they are likely to have more centralized, directive management structures, are less likely to create 'truces' about certain rules governing 'dress, manners and morals', are more likely to rely on blame rather than praise to orientate pupils, have more physical punishment, have lower levels of pupil co-option into school life, have 'tighter' and more alienating forms of organization, have teachers whose expectations are much lower for their pupils and have less developed schemes of primary/secondary school liaison. In all these ways, schools in Wales may be less effective in generating success than those elsewhere. When we assess the results of the comprehensive experiment in succeeding chapters, it must be made clear that the Welsh comprehensive system that was the model for our Treliw schools was not one that is marked by conspicuous success. Given a different educational history and different traditions of what the normal neighbourhood comprehensive school of Wales was supposed to be, Treliw comprehensives may also have been different in their organization, in their goals and in their effectiveness.

Treliw's Education System and the Research Strategy

We had already been researching into the educational system of Treliw for a number of years before the chance came to evaluate the effectiveness of comprehensive schools in attaining their goals. Our early work was into the secondary modern sector and concentrated upon a group of nine schools which exhibited very different levels of outcome in terms of attendance, academic attainment and delinquency. Data collection across eight schools of information on pupil background, pupil attitudes and school processes was undertaken and two of the schools were subject to an especially long period of attention taking a number of years, as we sought to understand the potentially causal role of school process and also generate further ideas for future work. This work is reported elsewhere (Reynolds, 1975 and 1976; Reynolds *et al*, 1987).

In 1973, five secondary modern schools and two other grammar schools were combined to form two new comprehensives. In both cases, the base of the new school was the former grammar school, which functioned in both cases as the site for years 2–5 and for the schools' sixth forms. Both comprehensives employed a lower school — former secondary modern schools — to house their first years. Both headteachers of the grammar schools became the headteachers of the comprehensive schools. Both comprehensives were split site.

Because we had 'blanket tested' the entire communities' primary schools when pupils were in their final term in summer 1974, in order to gain information for our first study and simply because we wanted a baseline against which any educational changes could be assessed, we had data on the pupil intake into the two comprehensive schools and into the selective system of a grammar school and two secondary moderns situated elsewhere in Treliw. This information covered pupil reading ability on two tests (Daniels and Diack, 1974; Watts and Vernon, 1947), mathematical ability (Vernon, 1971), personality (Eysenck, 1965) and non–verbal ability (Raven, 1960). Pupils that we had tested went as only the second intake to the two comprehensives or to the selective system that continued its normal functioning for four more years until it too went comprehensive.

We must be honest to the reader about the disadvantages of utilizing this data. Firstly, our early data collection was focussed upon boys, since we were initially concerned only with delinquency which was then in official statistics an overwhelmingly male offence. This study mostly has data on the differences between the two systems in their effect upon boys. Although all the data collection on school processes was on the schools as functioning and therefore mixed sex institutions, and although there is no evidence that school system effects are different for groups of boys as against girls, we in this study are again 'a no-woman's land' (Acker, 1982). Our third study comparing two comprehensive schools, begun in 1980 and finished in 1982, is not restricted in its focus by the nature of the intake data as we are here and gives girls' experience of school its proper place in the educational picture.

Secondly, our range of data about each pupil is more restricted than we would have liked. Other studies have shown academic, personality *and* social/family factors as important predictors of school outcomes at 15 (for example, Davie *et al*, 1972; Douglas, 1968), yet we have, of course, no social or family data that is specific to each child. Such data did exist in the primary school record cards which were transferred to the secondary school with our pupils but our findings were that it was out of date, sometimes wrong, often superseded by events (particularly by unemployment at this time in Treliw) and always collected only on the occupation of the father. Furthermore, it was impossible to assess occupation from many of the record cards because of imprecision of description. Quite how other researchers have been able to use such data remains unclear to us.

What we did have, though, was 1971 Census data on a large range of variables describing the catchment areas of the two systems. At a group level, then, we had a wide range of the social background data that we lacked at individual level and inspection of the two systems' catchment area data shows such homogeneity that the absence of *individual* social data is unlikely to be a source of any bias.

Thirdly, our selective system in Treliw is marked by an above average proportion of pupils getting grammar school places. Whereas nationally in the early to mid 1970s between 26 per cent and 29 per cent of pupils in the selective system went to grammar school (Gray *et al*, 1984), our cohort's proportion was over 41 per cent (42 out of 101 pupils). This makes our study atypical in an important respect and, given that pupils at grammar school are likely to do better than similar pupils at secondary moderns, may bias our results unfairly in favour of the selective system.

Fourthly, we look in this study at only the second ever intake into the comprehensive schools of our area, with the result that any problems or underperformance of the system may be attributable to either recency factors or to systemic factors that are a pure reflection of the systems' novelty. Simply, the settling down of school organizations in their early years may produce a particularly unfavourable response to their clients' needs.

That this 'newness' of the schools has generated an unfair portrait of their usual more mature functioning we doubt. Recent comprehensives in the NCB study did as well as more established ones (Fogelman and Holden, 1983, p. 8). Our intake was the second, not the first, into the schools. Also, since the selective system's staff knew that their system was imminently going comprehensive and since their school year 1977–78 was heavily disrupted by meetings and other preparation for the comprehensive reorganization of 1978, the selective system was also likely to be performing substantially below its true or real level of effectiveness.

We must alert the reader then to the disadvantages of this particular research area and of our cohort in terms of scientific adequacy. Whilst there is no existing evidence that boys are differently affected by comprehensives than girls and whilst the absence of individual data on social background is no handicap to us (as we show in chapter 4), the high proportion of pupils in grammar schools, the disadvantaged community, the atypicality of the Welsh educational system, the traditional nature of Welsh secondary schools and the bi-partitism that survived in Wales are all areas where our research atypicality must be admitted openly. Whilst England has been able to develop comprehensives out of grammar schools and secondary modern schools that were moving closer together in their curriculum and organization, it has taken Wales a decade merely to fuse these old traditions together. Whilst England tried to develop a *comprehensive* tradition, Wales has had to be content with getting its schools to a position where such a tradition might be begun.

In our defence, though, this study has a large number of strengths which, in our view, outweigh the potentially damaging effects of some of the above weaknesses. Ever since Campbell and Stanley (1963) wrote their classic treatise on experimental and quasi-experimental research designs, many social scientists, particularly in America, have advocated the use of true experiments as sources of data on which to judge the effectiveness of different programme or policy alternatives (for example, Kennedy, 1981; Gilbert and Mosteller, 1972). Ideally the experiment should involve the random assignment of individuals to a policy 'treatment', with the remainder of the sample getting either another policy or no policy at all, functioning as a control group to be compared on various policy outcomes with the treatment group (for example, Gilbert, Light and Mosteller, 1975). Such experiments although highly prevalent in medical science (see Cochrane, 1972), have been much rarer in social or educational research — local control of schools, the tendency of policy reforms to spread quickly, professional unwillingness to permit evaluation and the lack (particularly in Britain) of those skilled in this research tradition have all been factors holding back development of this research methodology.

Approximations to experiments or what are known as 'quasi experiments' have become therefore something of a substitute for the real thing and as such have numerous enthusiasts (for example, Cook and Campbell, 1975; Bronfennbrenner, 1979), some of whom view them as 'experiments of nature'. In this strategy, *non* randomly selected groups are the control for the policy treatment, ideally similar on all the background variables which may affect the outcomes that are being assessed. If groups are not thus similar, analysis of covariance or other statistical techniques are used to equate statistically groups which are known to differ. Whilst making comparisons between groups may still be difficult if differences between groups on variables other than those covaried have a large effect, quasi-experiments as Madaus, Airasian and Kellaghan (1980, p. 56) note, '. . . endeavour to approximate a true experimental strategy, so that causal inferences about treatments may be made with confidence'.

In this study, it is clear that ours is not a true experiment, with the random allocation of one group to comprehensives with the other selective school group as a control. Neither is it merely a quasi-experiment, since it was ultimately a random or chance factor (the distance of the modern schools from the grammar school) which prevented the selective system from going comprehensive along with the other, more conveniently located, schools elsewhere in Treliw. Finances were simply not available for the new buildings that the selective system would have required to go comprehensive.

Whatever the precise description of our research methodology may be, the chance treatment of one group of pupils in a different way to that of another group of identical pupils, both groups living in a ten mile area of the same community, is a research opportunity unknown within the research traditions established on comprehensivization.

This experiment has numerous advantages over other studies that have attempted to assess comprehensive school effectiveness. Firstly, it is of cohort design, so that the increment in each pupil's attainment and behaviour can be assessed, unlike cross sectional studies where different pupils represent the input and output in the different schools. Since input cohorts may be different because of population movement, social change or change in levels of parental preferences from what output cohorts were when they were inputs, unreliable estimates of school effects may follow.

Secondly, our two systems took the full ability range from their catchment areas and were in no way creamed by surviving 'super grammar schools' as in many areas (see Gray, Jesson and Jones, 1984). Although there was minimal creaming to independent schools (Director of Education's estimate was ten pupils per year), to a Roman Catholic school (approximately fifteen pupils) and to a Welsh medium school (twenty-eight in 1974), this total of about fifty pupils from an age cohort of 1381 pupils (703 boys) in total in summer 1974 is trivial by comparison with that reported in other studies. Since the Catholic school was not regarded locally as being replete with academic talent, the cohort that we tested was of the full ability range, differentiating this study from others.

Thirdly, our two systems took from defined catchment areas with no system of parental choice of school being used, unlike many other areas where parental choice systems are often superimposed over a neighbourhood school catchment area policy (as in London). Since parental choice systems make comparisons of school systems extremely difficult (since schools of similar intake ability may still have parents of potentially very different 'interest' in proportion to whether they have specifically requested a particular school or simply been allocated it), we have no such problem in this research study. We can relate our schools to our catchment areas with ease.

Fourthly, our community itself was relatively homogeneous by comparison with other areas of more heterogeneous class structure. Our preliminary investigation of census data on the catchment areas of the two systems showed a virtually identical picture on social and environmental variables. As we shall see later, by the standards of all existing research we have schools of similar social backgrounds.

Fifthly, the education authority and the teacher's unions agreed to our request for research access and granted unusually free access to schools, subject to the agreement of the headteachers of the schools. In just the same way as our first study, no conditions were placed on our access, no vetting of research instruments was required and no modification to the research programme was required at any stage. This openness is unique in research on this topic.

Sixthly, we were able to collect a range of data about the outcomes from our schools that is also unique in a study of this kind. Information on pupil reading ability, locus of control, attitudes to school and self conceptions was collected in the fourth year of schooling, and information on the examination results of the cohort was obtained in the fifth year. Although information on job destination and 'A' level grades is of less relevance since the selective system had gone comprehensive itself by the time our pupils featured in these statistics, this was also collected. The attendance rates of different schools and the names of all members of the sample who became officially delinquent were also obtained. Information was obtained on a range of cognitive and affective or social outcomes, without the concentration on merely the cognitive that has marked much work in this area.

Seventhly, we were able to collect a wide range of data on the internal processes of our systems that is also unique — indeed, studies of this issue have been notable for the absence of *any* process data on factors within schools that may be responsible for differential success (for example, Gray, McPherson and Raffe, 1983). Drawing on our early work which sub-divided the school into sub-areas of interest (Reynolds et al, 1987; Reynolds, 1982b) and looking at extra sub-areas and extra items in each sub area as we explain in chapter 5, we were able to follow the cohort in its early years (1974–76) through the schools. A gap of about a year without contact (1977) was followed by contact after that time through the testing and data collection programme in 1978 and 1979. Contact with the two comprehensives was also maintained after 1979 until 1982 in an attempt to compare the two schools with a third, highly-successful school in Treliw. Our illuminative process data, then, combine with our rigorous scientific strategy to generate a research study that in many ways exemplifies the good methodological practice required in studies of this topic.

Eighthly, we are reporting in this study on pupils who actually left school in 1979 or 1981, giving us the considerable advantage of recency by comparison with the studies of the National Children's Bureau (whose pupils left in 1974) or the Scottish studies (whose pupils left in 1975 or 1976). Whilst this recency of our data does mean that the comprehensive schools were facing social conditions such as youth unemployment that were largely unknown before, the changes that seem to have occurred in the comprehensive sector in the late 1970s can be tapped by this study in ways that cannot be done in other studies.

Ninthly, there was no evidence of any moving of parents to gain or avoid particular schools or systems throughout the entire decade of the 1970s. This simply has never been a Welsh tradition.

Conclusions

By contrast with the studies we have reviewed in chapter 2, we are in the fortunate position of being able to offer definitive answers to the questions that other researchers have been unable to answer. Our comprehensives are recent, taking the full ability range, uncreamed, without parental choice complications and of very similar social composition to pupils attending the ongoing selective system. We have data on the sample before and after their school experience, over four years, of the two systems and we also have a decade's worth of knowledge about the internal school processes in the area.

Our social and economic atypicality in terms of community structure, our provision of a high proportion of grammar school places and the nature of past Welsh educational traditions do, however, limit the generalizability of our studies. Whereas existing studies of this issue often have high external validity because of the typicality of their schools but low internal validity because of their weak research methodology, we have weak external validity because of school atypicality but strong internal validity. It is for the reader to judge how we compare with the research effort that has gone before us.

Chapter 4

The Effectiveness of Comprehensive and Selective Schooling

Everyone knows that comprehensives are allright for the clever kids. Its the duller ones that suffer.

(Treliw parent)

We have so far attempted to describe the history of comprehensive schooling in Britain, to account for its introduction as Labour Government policy and also to outline the research evidence which in general shows comprehensive schooling as having failed to attain the goals that have been posited for it.

In the last chapter we outlined the nature of our research community, its history and its present social characteristics which seem to be those typical of a traditional, respectable, collectivist working class community suffering from high levels of economic disadvantage but not possessed of the pockets of personal pathology typical of certain other poor urban areas, such as the Camberwell area of London with its high level of psychiatric disturbance as described in the Rutter *et al* (1979) survey. The research design for our work within this community we argued to have a considerable number of advantages in the attempt to assess the relative effectiveness of comprehensive schooling. This chapter now goes on to present our results on the attainments of the two systems. Chapter 5 attempts to use our large volume of school process data in an attempt to explain *how* these results were generated. The sample sizes on which analysis is based are 101 pupils in the selective system (forty-two in the grammar school) and 227 pupils in the two comprehensives (113 and 114 pupils each).

Individual Intake and Outcome Data

We noted earlier that we had collected a wide range of data on the intakes of pupils into the two systems in 1974, covering their personality, verbal ability (on the more 'easy' test of Daniels and Diack as well as on the more 'difficult' Watts-Vernon test to give us a sensitivity for the ability of slower learners), mathematical ability and non-verbal ability or intelligence.

These test scores were, we believed from our assessment of the research literature, good predictors of the social and academic outcomes of the schooling process and we therefore wanted to ensure that any variation in performance on the predictors by the intakes into the two systems should be taken into account before any comparison of the systems' effectiveness was made. Table 2 shows the two systems' results in terms of the performance of their intake cohorts on these predictor variables:

Table 2: 1974 Cohort Intake Data for Selective and Comprehensive Systems

	Selective		Comprehensive		T value/significance level	
	Mean	SD	Mean	SD		
Extraversion	16.97	5.05	17.38	5.63	−0.63	n.s.
Neuroticism	13.49	5.69	13.20	4.83	0.47	n.s.
Reading (D & D)	36.80	12.51	35.94	12.57	0.58	n.s.
Reading (WV)	16.55	6.88	16.52	7.14	0.05	n.s.
Maths	23.85	10.73	21.98	10.29	1.50	n.s.
Intelligence	37.79	11.13	34.64	12.82	2.14	n.s.

It is clear from an examination of these data that there are quite minimal differences in the mean intakes into the two systems and in the distribution of pupil scores as measured by the standard deviations. Differences in the mean scores of the intakes into the two systems are in evidence on the mathematics and intelligence tests yet of course on these tests as well as on the others the standard deviation or spread of the scores in the samples shows that there is much greater variation *within* each system's sample of pupils than there is *between* the samples of the two systems. By comparison with all the existing research studies we reviewed in chapter 2, we are in the scientifically enviable position of having a selective and comprehensive system with very similar intake characteristics in terms of the ability and personality of pupils.

Our outcome data was collected in the summer term of 1978, after our pupils had experienced four years of the two different systems. It included an indicator of academic attainment, the Edinburgh Reading Test measure of verbal ability, which we used as a surrogate for the examination results in public examinations that were available at the end of the fifth year of schooling. The test used was that appropriate for the age group in question (stage 4, for ages 12–16) and was of established validity and reliability. Scores of individual pupils were age adjusted to generate what we call an 'ERT' score and division of the raw, non-age adjusted scores into the five sub-divisions reflecting different skill performances was also undertaken.

The non-cognitive or affective or what some call social outcomes of schooling were measured in two respects. Firstly, two tests of pupil attitudes to school were given — the School Organization Index (called by us 'Attitude to School 1') and the School Climate Index (called by us 'Attitude to School 2') designed by Finlayson. These aim to tap pupil perceptions of their school environment, of teacher behaviour, of peer group behaviour and of the tone and flexibility of the school organization. The first scale sub-divides into two scales that measure school organisation and the second sub-divides into four scales measuring emotional tone, task orientation, teacher concern and social control. The two tests have been widely used and are of demonstrated reliability (Finlayson, 1970).

The second non-cognitive area we attemptd to tap was the pupils' locus of control, a concept which refers to the degree to which individuals feel that they have personal control over the events that happen to them. Individuals who feel that their own behaviour is responsible for their success are said to hold an internal locus of control — those who see life as being dependent upon luck, chance, fate or others actions are said to hold an external locus of control. This construct has recently become extensively utilised as a means of explanation of differing pupil performance on a wide variety of academic and social 'outcomes' of education (see Lefcourt, 1976). We utilized the Intellectual Achievement Responsibility Questionnaire designed by Crandall and his associates in 1965 as our measurement of this construct — again, it is of 'moderate reliability' as described by its designers and has been extensively utilized, particularly in the United States of America, on pupils of age groups similar to our cohort.

It is important to appreciate that our 'attitude to school' data and our locus of control data are, in a sense, 'process' data as well as measurements of the actual outcomes of the schooling systems. Given the extensive literature linking attitude to school and academic attainment (for example, Banks and Finlayson, 1973) and linking, as with the Crandall (1965) study, locus of control and attainment, both these outcomes may well also serve as processual determinants of other outcomes like academic attainment. Also, given the likely impact of academic attainment upon pupil attitude to school and pupil perception of the wider social environment, the social outcomes may also be partly determined (in a process of interactive feedback) by the academic outcomes.

We noted earlier that there were minor differences in some of the ability and personality characteristics of the intakes into the two systems. Although it seemed unlikely that such small differences would have much effect in biassing the selective/comprehensive comparison in favour of the selective system because of its more academically advantaged intake, it was clearly necessary to statistically 'take out' the effect of the intakes upon the outcome scores of the two systems (ERT, Attitude and Locus of Control actual 'raw scores' can be seen in Appendix 1 for the whole sample).

We calculated, therefore, for the sample as a whole the relationship at an individual level between each intake measure and each outcome measure, whether academic or social (for full details see Appendix 2). Interestingly, the tests where the comprehensive pupils and the selective pupils were performing at similar levels on intake (those measuring verbal ability) proved to have the best relationship with the outcomes — on mathematics and on the intelligence test, the relationships were considerably weaker.

The effects of this when we predicted, using the whole sample relationships and all the intake measures in a multiple regression analysis, the outcome scores was then to generate *predicted* scores for the two systems that were very similar (see table 3). Looking at the residuals, however, it is clear that the comprehensive school pupils performed much worse on all the outcomes than one might have expected at age 11, the disparity being marked on reading ability, very marked on locus of control and again marked on the first of the attitude scales relating to school organization. If we compare the difference or residual scores for the two systems with the spread of the scores as measured by the standard deviations to place the difference scores in some sort of perspective, it is clear that the reading score differences and the attitude scale 1 differences are reasonably marked by comparison with the overall differences of the sample children when all are compared with each other. The locus of control difference scores, by the same comparison, indicate very marked system effects by comparison with the differences occurring amongst the children in the sample as a whole.

Table 3: Actual and Predicted Outcome Scores for Two Systems

| | Selective | | Comprehensive | | Residuals | |
	Actual	Predict	Actual	Predict	Sel	Comp
Age ERT	100.27	95.62	94.50	96.88	+4.85	−2.38
Att. to School 1	70.78	69.18	63.38	67.32	+1.60	−3.94
Att. to School 2	55.98	55.83	54.28	54.36	+ .15	−0.08
Locus of Control	24.14	20.27	17.86	19.85	+3.87	−1.99

(Full details of regressions are to be found in Appendix 3).

Table 4: Residuals and Standard Deviations

| | Residuals | | Standard Deviation | |
	Selective	Comprehensive	Selective	Comprehensive
Age ERT	+4.65	−2.38	14.51	17.08
Att. to School 1	+1.60	−3.94	14.62	14.20
Att. to School 2	+ .15	−0.08	12.52	13.66
Locus of Control	+3.87	−1.99	3.80	4.37

It might be possible to argue that the comprehensive system's poorer performance was simply due to our not having adequately tapped the extent of the disadvantage of its intake at age 11 due to the absence of data on the social characteristics of the individual pupils. However, inspection of 1971 census data on the social characteristics of the two system's catchment areas three years before our pupils entered their schools shows virtually identical social conditions existed for both systems, as Table 5 shows. Whilst the selective system's catchment area is slightly more advantaged in terms of social class composition, if we look at the proportion of one parent families, household amenities and housing overcrowding, the *comprehensive* system is more advantaged. In view of this data, it is difficult for us to believe that the

Table 5: Catchment Areas of the Two Systems

	Selective	Comprehensive
Average Household Size	2.94	2.97
Percentage pop. in social class one/two	9.7	8.2
Percentage pop. in social class five	15.7	16.2
Percentage households one parent families	8.6	8.1
Percentage households lacking one or more amenity	57.6	50.0
Percentage households overcrowded		
(more than one person per room)	5.7	5.5

Source: 1971 Census.

inclusion of social data on the individual pupils would have accounted for the comprehensive system's poor performance in ways that individual intellectual data does not.

Furthermore, there is no doubt that the limited range of individual intake data that we possess does actually explain a relatively high proportion of the variation in individual's outcome scores. Taking our ERT score as an example, the intake variables generated an R^2 value of 0.62 for their relationship with the age adjusted reading scores that we have concentrated our analysis on (for details of regressions for all major outcome variables, see Appendix 3). Looking at the recent studies of comprehensive and selective schools summarized in Cox and Marks (1983), we are actually explaining a similar amount of variance in outcomes to these other major studies — Steedman (1983) has an R^2 value of 0.80 for a combination of seven intake variables against academic outcomes, Cox and Marks (1983) have a value of 0.85 for five input variables against examination attainments and the Department of Education and Science (1983) gives values of 0.77 for six input variables against high examination attainments.

We collected further data on each individual that we are reporting shortly elsewhere. This covered the further social or affective outcome of the pupil's self conceptions or views of themselves, their characters and their capabilities, measured by a specially constructed questionnaire (Reynolds and Murgatroyd, forthcoming). We also collected data on the social status of each individual child, in particular where the child comes from within the community.

This further data will answer the question of the extent which the comprehensives developed the further social aspects of their pupils, and the extent to which the comprehensives did well or badly with pupils from different status groups.

Our third set of data focusses upon the examination attainments of the pupils in the schools when they sat their 'O' levels or CSE examinations at the end of their fifth year of schooling. Since our selective system had itself gone comprehensive by summer 1979, this analysis compares our pupils who had five years of comprehensive education with those who had four years of selective education and only one year of the new comprehensive school.

Our fourth set of data covers the occupational destinations and, in some cases, 'A' level grades of pupils from the two systems collected from summer 1979 to summer 1981.

Group Outcome Data

This was collected on the entire cohort of pupils in their fourth year and covered their delinquency and their attendance at school. In order to see if any differences in these social outcomes were produced by differences in the social background of the pupils entering the schools, data was used as above from the 1971 Census on social conditions in the catchment areas of the two comprehensives and of the selective system.

Looking at delinquency first, defined as a guilty court finding or an official caution, the comprehensive system generated forty-three delinquents in total, out of 227 pupils, a rate of 18.9 per cent. The selective system generated ten offenders out of 101 pupils, a 9.9 per cent rate. Also, it is important to note that whilst the selective system generated only ten *offences* by its ten offenders over the four years 1974–78, the comprehensive system actually generated seventy-three *offences* by its forty-three offenders.

On attendance, the comprehensive system's poorer performance is again marked. Using the attendance rates on fourth year pupils for the entire academic year 1977/78 calculated from form registers, the two comprehensive schools achieved rates of 75.2 per cent and 61.2 per cent respectively for their 113 and 114 sample pupils. The selective system — weighted for the differences in the number of pupils going to the three schools — achieved a rate of 78.8 per cent, some 10 per cent above the mean for the two comprehensive schools. The rate for the grammar school pupils (forty-two) was 81.2 per cent and that for the secondary modern school pupils was 79.4 per cent (twenty-nine pupils) and 74.7 per cent (thirty pupils). In our survey, then, the two secondary modern schools together were actually outperforming the comprehensive system. Inspection of our range of census data on social conditions in the catchment areas of the two systems does not suggest that these factors were responsible for these differences. Table 5 above showed this data for the two systems.

Again, it is simply very difficult to believe that the comprehensive system's slight excess proportion in social class five, or its slightly lower proportion of population in social class one could account for its inferior performance, particularly since it appears to be *less* socially deprived in its proportion of one parent families, its housing conditions and its overcrowding rate. There is also nothing in the available literature to suggest that the minor differences in the personality and ability scores of the pupil intakes could, even together with the social background data above, explain more than a small proportion of the difference between the systems in these social or affective outcomes. These differences we believe are almost completely due to school system effects.

So far, then, we have seen that the large differences between the two systems in their outcomes in terms of reading ability, attitudes to school and pupil perception of their personal power in affecting the wider environment are not explicable by the minor differences in the personality and ability of the pupils when they entered the systems four years earlier. Differences in the social background of the pupils gauged by the census data seem to be minimal, and neither the individual data nor the census data would seem able to explain the large differences in the two system's performance on our social outcomes of delinquency and attendance. Whilst the differences in reading ability and one of the attitude scales are not trivial in size, it is the differences in the social outcomes of delinquency, attendance, and locus of control that seem to be particularly marked.

As well as the data collected specifically at the end of the fourth year of schooling, other data exists that in general confirms the picture that we have painted above of the comprehensive's ineffectiveness by comparison with the selective system. An unpublished survey of police referrals to the Social Services Department of Treliw enabled us to look at the picture of delinquency for all pupils (boys and girls, older and younger pupils) in the two systems — in 1976, the two comprehensives' pupils generated 272 referrals, whilst the selective system generated only ninety-five. Again, these were generated by pupils from virtually identical backgrounds. Even taking into account the relative size of the two pupil groups (a ratio of 2.25:1) does not explain the differences.

Our pupils also feature in other sets of statistics that have been routinely collected in the county of which Treliw is a part. At 'A' level in 1981, of the pupils who had undergone four years of selective education plus three years in a comprehensive, 15.2 per cent were entered for an 'A' level subject — the two comprehensives figures were 17.9 per cent and 10 per cent, giving a lower mean total. Of the selective/comprehensive pupils, 63.8 per cent attained pass grades (A to E) as a proportion of the total entry — the two comprehensives scored 58.1 per cent and 57.3 per cent. For the selective/comprehensive pupils, 6.4 per cent of total grades were at an 'A' — for the two comprehensives, the figures were 3.2 per cent and 2.7 per cent. Again, the social and intellectual background of these 'A' level cohorts at intake would not seem able to explain differences of this magnitude.

We have also additional data on the examination performance of the two systems in 1976, two years before our pupils furnished us with outcome data. In the former year, the three communities feeding the selective system recorded figures of 41.5 per cent, 45 per cent and 48 per cent in the proportion of pupils with one or more 'O' levels or a CSE equivalent — the communities feeding the two comprehensive schools record figures of 39.2 per cent, 25.7 per cent, 34.9 per cent, 22.2 per cent, 26.1 per cent, 16.3 per cent, 50 per cent, 34.5 per cent, 23.3 per cent and 41.7 per cent. Only two of the comprehensive communities (where those pupils have had three years of comprehensive schooling) approach or surpass the figures attained by the communities whose pupils have spent the whole of their secondary experience (five years) in the selective system. Again, the social characteristics of the catchment areas are identical, as we saw in Table 5.

One last piece of information is provided by one of our own past projects on school attendance (Reynolds, 1977). Whilst attendance rates in the community of Treliw as a whole fell rapidly in the early 1970s, Table 6 shows that the fall was greatest for those pupils in the comprehensive system. System A, which was our selective system, held the fall to 4.4 per cent (for boys/girls and all pupils years 1–5). System B, (our comprehensives) which had gone comprehensive showed a fall of 6.4 per cent. Again, the selective and comprehensive catchment areas are identical on the range of 1971 Census data, as we have seen earlier.

Table 6: The Effects of Comprehensive Education on Attendance

	Autumn 1972	*Autumn 1974*
System A (Grammar/secondary moderns)	87.9	83.5
System D (Goes comprehensive 1973)	88.4	82.0

Source: Reynolds (1977) p. 67.

With Which Pupils Do Comprehensives Fail?

It is important for us now to consider which parts of the ability range the comprehensive school is failing to develop in both social and affective areas. Whereas the national discussion of this issue has almost uniformly concentrated upon whether high ability pupils are being adequately served in the comprehensive schools as they have purportedly been before in the selective system (for example, Stevens, 1980), our data in this study leads us toward very different conclusions about which portion of the ability range has been in this sense 'uneducated'.

For our analysis of different ability bands' experiences in the schools, we have split the entire population of 328 pupils into three ability bands — band A, (containing 128 pupils and representing the grammar school and the equivalent forms within the comprehensives), band B, (110 pupils representing the middle of the comprehensive ability range and the top or 'A' streams in the secondary moderns) and band C, (ninety pupils representing the 'B' streams of the secondary moderns and the bottom third of the comprehensive's ability range). Band A children were seen as potentially examination candidates in a range of subjects. Band B were viewed as candidates in perhaps a few subjects each, often at CSE level. Band C children were only seen as examination material in perhaps one, two or (more likely) in no subjects.

Band A represented 41 per cent of selective children and 38 per cent within the two comprehensives — band C, by contrast, covered 27 per cent of selective children and 28 per cent of comprehensive children.

If we look at age adjusted reading ability first, the results are as follows — for the top band pupils, the selective system score was a predicted 105.80, but the actual score attained was 113.35. For the two comprehensives, the predicted mean score was 104.95, but the actual score obtained was 108.06. For the bottom third of the ability range, the selective system prediction was 87.47 and the actual scores attained 87.14 — for the comprehensives, the prediction was 84.45 but the actual scores obtained were only 80.69. Middle band children were predicted 93.11 in the selective system and attained 94.15 — in the comprehensives, the prediction was for 94.35 and the scores attained only 90.69.

Moving on to look at the results for the locus of control scale, for selective top band pupils the prediction of 22.02 was exceeded by actual scores of 24.97. For similar comprehensive pupils, the prediction of 21.31 was matched by an actual score of 20.22. For bottom band selective pupils, the prediction of 18.83 was massively exceeded by an actual score of 23.11 — for bottom band comprehensive pupils, a prediction of 18.23 was massively undershot by an actual score of 15.76. Middle band pupils also showed large differences between the systems — for middle band pupils, the selective pupils' predicted score was 19.19 — the actual score obtained was 23.91. For comprehensive pupils, the predicted score was 19.55 — the actual score obtained only 16.96.

The two 'attitude to school' scales are the last set of individual level data that we consider here. On the first scale of attitudes to school organization, the top ability band was predicted 75.12 in the selective system and obtained 82.35, whereas the comprehensives prediction of 74.16 was only slightly exceeded at 75.24. For lower bands, the comprehensive prediction of 58.94 compares with an actual score of 54.85 — for the selective system, a prediction of 63.63 compares with a much lower actual score of 57.37. For middle ability children, the selective system prediction of 66.05 was matched by an actual score of 66.90 — for comprehensives, a prediction of 66.52 compares with a much lower actual score of 57.19.

The school climate scale — lastly — generates results as follows, since small differences in mean scores for the two groups of pupils overall hide more substantial differences in the performance of the different ability ranges. For high ability children, the selective prediction of 60.94 is outscored by an actual score of 64.40 — for comprehensives, a prediction of 60.30 is similarly matched by a score of 64.68. For bottom band children, a selective prediction of 50.89 compares with a lower score of 46.51 — for comprehensives, the prediction of 47.12 compares with a quite similar actual figure of 46.49. For the middle band, a selective prediction of 53.28 compares with a similar score of 52.90 — a comprehensive prediction of 53.65 compares with an actual score of a much lower 49.10.

In order to assess the overall balance of advantage to the selective system in performance, we calculated a score for each of the outcome measures that reflects the difference between the two systems in their performance (i.e. selective actual minus predicted, minus comprehensive actual minus predicted). Results can be seen in Table 7 for each ability band.

Table 7: Outcome Results by Ability Band — Selective Advantage Over Comprehensive

	ERT	Locus of control	Attitude 1	Attitude 2
Band 1 (128 pupils)	+4.44	+4.04	+6.15	−.92
Band 2 (110 pupils)	+4.70	+7.31	+10.18	+4.17
Band 3 (90 pupils)	+3.43	+6.75	−2.17	−3.75

Overall, it must be clear that the differences between the systems in their performance with the different ability bands are quite marked. The comprehensive's worst performance is with the middle ability bands, where their deficit on reading, locus of control and the two attitude scales is greatest. The comprehensive's performance with the high ability pupils is mixed — poor on reading, relatively good on the locus of control scale and a performance on the two attitude scales that is intermediate between that of the other two ability ranges. The comprehensive's performance with the lower part of the ability range is also mixed — relatively good on reading ability, relatively good on the attitude scales where on both of them the comprehensives actually out perform the selective system and quite poor on the locus of control scale. The small numbers that are in the different bands in the two systems, the possible effect of 'outlier' or extreme scores upon these system means and the usual effects of pupil errors should all be kept in mind when assessing the possible significance of these findings.

We have two further sets of data that enable us to assess which part of the ability range was responsible for the failure of the comprehensive system in its general levels of effectiveness — that on the attendance rate of one of the comprehensives, the grammar school and one of the secondary moderns analyzed by individual form, and that on the distribution of delinquency through the ability range by the end of the schooling process that the pupils had undergone. To look at delinquency first, the selective system was notable for the relatively even spread of offenders through the ability range — four (out of forty-two) were at the grammar and six (out of fifty-nine) were in the other two thirds of the ability range. In the two comprehensive schools, the bottom two-thirds of the ability range generated thirty-two (out of forty-three) offenders, a proportion higher than the distribution of pupil numbers would have suggested to be likely. In view of small numbers, it seemed inadvisable to undertake a more detailed analysis of the two lower ability bands.

Our last piece of information, as we noted earlier, is on the detailed attendance rates of pupils in classes of two of the three selective schools and in one of the comprehensives. The comprehensive obtained 84.5 per cent attendance with its top band pupils in the Christmas term of their fourth year — the grammar obtained 85.4 per cent with its top band pupils. For middle band pupils, the comprehensive obtained 66.4 per cent for the same time period, whereas the top band of the secondary modern obtained no less than 91.5 per cent attendance. For the bottom band comprehensive pupils, the figure obtained was 49.2 per cent — the secondary modern school obtained a figure of 83.4 per cent for comparable pupils, an overperformance of about 25 per cent and 35 per cent for both the bottom two ability bands by comparison with the comprehensive school. With both these group based outcome measures, it is the inferior performance of the comprehensive school with the bottom two-thirds of the ability range that is most marked, whilst the schools seem to have held their top ability band pupils to a delinquency rate and an attendance rate very similar to that of the grammar school.

Conclusions

We have presented a large amount of data in this chapter which we now summarize in point fashion:

1   The comprehensive and the selective system are receiving pupils of similar ability and personality at age 11, taken from very similar social backgrounds.
2   Statistical adjustments for the slightly superior intellectual quality of the selective system's intakes do not dispose of the large differences in the academic and social outcomes from the two systems.
3   These differences seem to be marked in the areas of delinquency, attendance and in the locus of control of the pupils. They seem to be less marked in the areas of verbal ability and in attitudes to school.
4   The differences which we have shown for our cohort of pupils from 1974 and 1978 are supported by further data showing system differences in 'A' level results, 'O' level results, attendance rates for all pupils and delinquency rates for all pupils.
5   The comprehensive schools' poor performance is due — looking at the individual data — to particularly poor results with the middle third of the ability range who in the selective system attended the top streams of the secondary modern schools. Performance with the top and bottom third of the ability range is more mixed.
6   Looking at our group data, it is the bottom two-thirds of the ability range that can be assessed as being responsible for the comprehensives poor performance on delinquency and the bottom third of the ability range that does particularly poorly on attendance. The com-

prehensive system holds, by contrast, the performance of the higher ability children to attendance and delinquency levels similar to those of the selective system's grammar school.

Our next chapter looks at the internal organization of the two systems in an attempt to account for and explain these findings. Our conclusions about our own work and the implications of it for national policy and discussion of the comprehensive system are to be found in our final chapter.

Chapter 5

School Processes within the Two Systems

I sometimes think that running a comprehensive school in the late 1970's is rather akin to being a Church Bishop in Albania.

(Comprehensive headteacher)

Following our presentation of results and findings in chapter 4, we will attempt in this chapter two related tasks. Firstly, we will try to explain how the *social* outcomes of the comprehensive system came to be worse than its *academic* outcomes by comparison with the selective system and, secondly, we will try to explain why the ineffectiveness of the comprehensive system is particularly marked with the middle ability band (as on some of our measures) and with the two lower ability bands (as on our other measures).

The information that we have on school processes was collected by us prior to any analysis of the data on the outcomes from the schools to ensure that it was as objective as possible. Further information on the early history of the comprehensives after their founding in 1973, on their functioning in 1974, 1975 and 1976, and on the changes that have taken place in them since the late 1970s was collected as part of the ongoing programme of work in Treliw.

The Comprehensive's 'Settling Down' Phase

Although our group of pupils was the second cohort to enter the new comprehensive schools, the experience of the two schools prior to that date had not been an entirely happy or harmonious one — reverberations, dissatisfactions and conflicts from the period prior to changeover in 1973 and from the first year of operation were still affecting the comprehensives' capacity to become effective educational environments. Firstly, joining the staff groups of one grammar school with in each case those of three secondary modern schools was a difficult process. For about the first six months, little cross group interaction took place — friendship groups that had been created in the old, smaller schools were, if anything, made even stronger in the new comprehensives as teachers arrived uncertain of the goals or means that the comprehensives would reflect. Pupils, too, appeared to have remained mostly in their former peer groups for six to nine months, and in both comprehensive schools there were not infrequent fights between groups of pupils from the different secondary schools in the first months. These had ceased, however, by the time of the arrival of our 1974 intake, although the pupil and teacher sub-cultures still appeared partially organized on the basis of their prior educational experiences in different schools.

Secondly, the actual process of going comprehensive had itself generated discontent and friction both before, during and after reorganization. Both headteachers were allocated what they regarded as very generous allocations of 'points' for distribution amongst staff — in both schools, there was widespread discontent about who was awarded points, the process of decision making about the allocation and the communication of decisions to those teaching in the schools. Discontent had been further aroused by inadequate consultation between the two grammar schools and the schools that they were to receive, by inadequate liaison on curricular and other matters between the schools and by the general orientation of a process which the secondary modern staff viewed as a grammar school take over of their schools. So great was the fear that the special contributions of the secondary modern teachers would be ignored in the comprehensives that in one of the two schools, some three-quarters of the former boys secondary modern teachers lobbied to be allowed to stay with their former headteacher in the new lower school of the comprehensive which was located in their building. The domination of the head of department role by former grammar school teachers — they got initially approximately two-thirds of these jobs across the two schools — and the need to protect the salaries of senior staff involved in the changeover, which led directly to the expansion of the pastoral year tutor role as a niche for them, also had aroused discontent amongst grammar school staff (who viewed their academic 'inferiors' arriving on large salaries) and among former secondary modern junior staff who were not so protected as their senior colleagues.

The Comprehensive Advantages

The schools into which our pupils went in 1974 therefore had still not settled after the tribulations of the reorganization of the previous year. Nevertheless, those pupils going to the two comprehensive schools did have a number of what can only be regarded as advantages — their teachers were better paid, since both the comprehensives' teaching staffs were being paid a social priority allowance because both comprehensive schools just crept over the qualification line in terms of proportion of pupils on free school meals. In the selective system, only one of the three schools — the smallest secondary modern — had teaching staff qualifying for the payment. If the comprehensive system should have benefitted then in having the more committed, potentially more stable and more generously motivated group of teachers that the payments were meant to encourage, the physical plant of that system should also have given it considerable advantages. Two of the three selective schools, the secondary modern schools, were in buildings regarded by the education authority as entirely unsuitable. Whilst the grammar school's buildings were regarded as more adequate (adequate enough in fact to permit it to become the lower school of a comprehensive system in time), the selective sector was not favoured in its building stock — although one of the comprehensives was in marginally unsuitable buildings, the other comprehensive was new and purpose built. Also, both the former secondary modern schools were deficient in facilities which both the new comprehensive schools possessed — the former had no science laboratories, no language teaching facilities, inadequate physical education facilities, inadequate storage provision, no domestic science provision on site, no playing fields, completely outdoor sanitation, no self-contained canteen, no medical inspection room and inadequate staff accommodation. Support staff were more generously provided in the comprehensive system, in terms of a better ratio of secretarial help and laboratory assistants. One of the comprehensive schools was also purpose built as a community school, with use of school facilities, swimming baths etc. by a youth club and adult centre — no such close community involvement, which can only be regarded as beneficial, was built into the selective system. The comprehensives also had a better ratio of library books per pupil and were given a higher per pupil capitation allowance to help their early phase of development.

In its staffing too, the comprehensive system had been more generously provided for than the selective, although some of the potential that this gave for smaller class size was eroded because of the growth in the comprehensive schools of a middle management strata with reduced teaching loads. (The Deputy Heads in one of the comprehensives taught for only eight lessons a week). Nevertheless, average class size for core subjects in year 4 was twenty-eight and twenty-seven in the two secondary moderns and was twenty-seven in the grammar school — in the two comprehensives it was twenty-six and twenty-five.

The more generous staffing of the comprehensive system also enabled it to offer a range of subjects far above what was possible in the selective system, particularly for the bottom two-thirds of the ability range being offered in the latter a secondary modern curriculum. Whereas one of the secondary moderns, for example, offered English, mathematics, geography, history, art and craft, woodwork, science, religious education and domestic science together with physical education as its fourth year curriculum, one of the comprehensive schools, for example, offered all these subjects with the addition of physics, biology, computer studies, economics, commerce, geology, engineering theory, Italian, dress and design, music, Welsh, Welsh studies, technical drawing, metalwork and motor mechanics. Both comprehensive schools also had generously staffed remedial departments, well financed in capitation terms, by comparison with a complete absence of such specialist provision in the selective system's secondary modern schools.

Given these advantages, what factors seem to explain the comprehensive system's marked lack of success?

Organizational Problems

The two comprehensive schools were clearly of a considerably larger size than those of the selective system — one was of 1400 pupils and the other of 1300 pupils — and the existence of numbers of this kind, together with staff groups of over eighty, clearly imposed demands upon the schools' management teams that they found difficult to meet. Both headteachers were widely regarded as finding delegation difficult — since both had formerly been headteachers of grammar schools of approximately 500 pupils, they had been used to being able to centralize decision-making about all curriculum, discipline, pastoral and academic matters upon themselves. Whilst both delegated timetabling and pastoral/disciplinary matters to members of their senior management teams, academic and curricular matters were widely regarded as remaining highly centralized — indeed, one of the headteachers reported in the school handbook to parents that decisions about use of text books and equipment taken by heads of subject departments were only taken 'After I have decided what subjects are to be taught'.

Together with lack of delegation — which in one school went as far as the headteacher handing out stationery and textbooks to heads of subject departments — went a centralization of decision-making within the senior management teams of deputy heads and senior mistresses/masters. In both schools, members of these teams were regarded as spending much time in each others' company and as forming almost a clique that ran school life. The exclusion of the heads of year from these groups was something that intensely annoyed them and led to an increasing separation of the pastoral side from the academic side of school life.

Size of organization posed other problems for the two comprehensive schools. A larger site than the smaller selective schools meant that a much greater area of buildings had to be supervised and further increased the chances of pupils being able to truant after registration, either by hiding within the school or leaving it, together with increasing the likelihood of casual vandalism being perpetrated on school buildings. The staff groups, however, appeared increasingly reluctant in both schools to take on the needed supervisory role — the former grammar staff were unused to this exercise since it had not been necessary before comprehensivization when it had then been undertaken by prefects, and the former secondary modern staff who used to practise such control functions were in the process of redefining their role and functions to be more 'imparters of knowledge' than persons with academic *and* social functions. The size of the school units and the fact that both schools had separate lower schools also increased timekeeping problems for both pupils and staff — our estimate is that an average double lesson for a fourth year class was some three to four minutes shorter in the comprehensive schools because of the distance that staff and pupils had to travel. For lessons in the two lower schools involving teachers from the main comprehensive buildings, this shortfall of time was probably over twice that for the lessons in the main schools.

The effects of size factors, the felt lack of involvement of staff in decision taking, the effects of initial problems in settling down different staff and pupil groups and the initial uncertainty and confusion as to the precise goals of the new schools all led to what can only be termed a serious fragmentation of the educational environment provided in the two comprehensive schools. The staff groups — initially *personally* fragmented — appear to have become even less *ideologically* cohesive as our cohort passed through the school in the middle 1970s, as groups of teachers responded in somewhat different ways to the stresses that the schools were experiencing. Whilst some teachers gravitated towards more authoritarian disciplinary stances, others retreated or withdrew the investment of their emotional energy from school life, distancing themselves behind various barriers. Not until the late 1970s — after our pupils had left — did these ideological differences begin to diminish as consensus emerged.

Consistency of rule enforcement in the schools consequently suffered — some staff began to apply rules more strictly whilst others let more misdemeanours pass. Expectations of pupils' attainments and behaviour also became more variegated. High levels of staff turnover — 12 per cent in the comprehensive system between 1976 and 1978, compared to only 4 per cent in the selective system — faced pupils again with an inconsistency of demands from a changing staff group. If the three factors of continuity, consistency and cohesion are associated with control, then it is not difficult to understand the problems that the comprehensives faced in the social control of their pupils, since they lacked all three.

What were absent from the comprehensives were routine administrative procedures for ensuring that these large organizations did not fragment but instead showed cohesion and consistency. Because of size, turnover of staff, split sites, the pastoral/academic division of staff and the initial heterogeneity of the staff groups, the involvement of teachers in some form of collective decision making or other consensus-making arrangements would have been necessary but no such opening up of school administration to the teachers was pursued by either headteacher. Centralization of decision-making was more prevalent in one of the comprehensives than in the other but in both, leadership was seen by the staff as remote, non-expressive, non-responsive and unknowledgeable about the nature of school problems. The ethos of headteacher/staff decision-making is perhaps best captured by the headteacher's letter to parents in the Form One Parents Handbook from one of the schools:

Administration of the School

As headmaster of the whole comprehensive school, I am ultimately responsible for every aspect of the school's life. Since the school is so large some things normally done by a small school headmaster I delegate to other senior officers. Basically I am responsible for advising the governors and authority on the staffing of the school, decide (after taking advice from my senior staff and heads of department and the authority's advisers) on what should be taught (that is, the curriculum) and what teachers should teach it, what option choices should be offered in Form III, what jobs my officers should do, how we should use our rooms, allocating money for books and equipment, entry into colleges from the sixth form, standards in the school, the work of form teachers, all major academic problems, any other problems of a serious nature that my officers feel should be passed on to me.

The deputy head, Mr. X, my first deputy, deputises for me in my absence and is responsible for general discipline in upper school, makes out the internal examination timetable and the supervision lists for the WJEC examinations and is responsible for attendance in the whole complex.

The academic deputy, Miss Y, my second deputy, is responsible for the making of the timetable for the whole school according to my forward planning, for dealing with classes whose teachers may be ill on certain days, for oversight of entries for the WJEC examinations and for assisting in the whole school's general administration.

There were, of course, other mechanisms than participation in decision making that could have ensured greater consensus of goals and means in the academic and behavioural areas. Neither school had a staff handbook and neither school used a noticeboard system to ensure that members of staff knew who was absent on whatever business.

Staff meetings were relatively infrequent. Neither headteacher spent much time with ordinary non-management 'line' teachers, so the personal contact that could have ensured transmission of information and led to a greater consensus on goals was absent.

Since neither at a relational level, nor an organizational level, was it possible for cohesion and consistency of goals/means to be encouraged, the fragmentation of attitudes/behaviour and the headteacher/staff split inevitably led to a degree of personal friction. Cliques, formed around ideological positions taken by the different groups of staff, often became peer or friendship groups, meeting in different parts of the school or staff common room at breaktime or lunchtime. Whilst teachers in both schools might have gained support from the members of their group, the mutual support of the staff group for each other and the mutual control of each others' actions that comes from cohesion was noticeably absent.

The contrast with the selective sector was marked. There, staff groups were small — about sixteen in the secondary moderns for example. The groups had been in existence for some time, were not fragmented and were part of an educational system that had no goal confusion, being concerned with academic training in the grammar school and with social care in the modern schools. Numbers were small enough to ensure cohesion and consistency of approach. No formal organizational mechanisms were needed to generate a collectivity, since the three headteachers used charismatic, rather than bureaucratic, authority in their dealings with people. The system had continuity, consistency and was cohesive — it clearly also managed to be more effective in terms of social control.

Pastoral Care and Dealings with Problem Pupils

The overwhelming evidence from the comprehensives suggests that pastoral concerns were given a lower prominence than the attainment of academic results. This is, of course, easy to understand. In the community of Treliw, comprehensive education was always regarded as giving more children the chance of access to the examination streams of the former grammar schools, which would both be opened up and extended down the ability range. Political discussion of the issue of comprehensivization was always concerned with the instrumental academic benefit that it would bring to Treliw children — indeed, given the area's past concern to ensure that all able pupils got success by means of the grammar school, such a portrayal of the schools was inevitable. In the first year of the comprehensives, in fact, there were a noticeable number of visits from parents of former grammar school children who visited to ensure that, as one put it, 'our children aren't missing out'. We were also aware of governor and political pressure to ensure standards were maintained.

Both headteachers relinquished, therefore, their pastoral duties — in marked contrast to the headteachers of the two secondary moderns who viewed pastoral and academic matters as both of equal importance and who themselves aimed to undertake pastoral work, not merely delegating to other senior teachers.

The second major problem with pastoral care in the comprehensives — other than its de-emphasis by comparison with academic matters — was the administrative arrangements for operating it. The notion of the form teacher as the primary pastoral care mechanism, with year heads and then the senior mistress or deputy headteacher as an 'end-stop' for the most intractable, difficult or lengthy cases was difficult to work in practice; there was minimal guidance on which cases should be referred upwards by the form teacher, there were often lengthy delays between the emergence of a problem (disciplinary or personal) and its being dealt with by year heads and the procedure generated an increasingly split academic and pastoral responsibility within the schools. It also encouraged a tendency for the form teachers and other teachers to regard their role as basically imparters of knowledge, not as both pastoral and academic agents. The selective system, by contrast, had no specialist pastoral staff and no separation of the pastoral from the academic, viewing the form teacher as the sole pastoral agent, except for every rare referals up to the headteacher or his deputy (see Reynolds and Murgatroyd, 1980, for further data on bureaucratized pastoral care).

The difference between the two systems of education can perhaps best be illustrated by simply reporting our observations of three schools and their pastoral care arrangements and concern — the grammar school (with little pastoral care emphasis), the secondary modern schools (with major commitment to such care) and one of the comprehensives (similar to the grammar school in its lack of emphasis). These are now reported from our notebooks:

> *In the grammar school* — there is, as one might expect, no formal pastoral care system. (i.e. no career pastoral posts). In general, teachers in this school felt that they were employed to teach, not to act as pastoral counsellors — not opposed to counselling but to seeing it as part of the reasonable duty of a teacher.
>
> The headteacher and senior mistress are officially ultimately responsible for the pastoral care of pupils. Both of these members of staff expressed concern for the non-academic development of their pupils but as far as one could see there was little concrete action to back up this expressed concern.
>
> Theoretically the system in operation is: form teacher picks up any difficulties amongst pupils in his/her form. Academic difficulties dealt with by FT and subject teacher. Non-academic problems referred by FT to HM or senior mistress and through them to one of the outside agencies if deemed necessary.
>
> In fact my impression is that non-academic problems are presented to staff very infrequently not because they don't exist but because the school ethos is such that pupils feel that the school is not the appropriate place and staff not the appropriate people to bring forward problems — even those related to school.
>
> This may be the result of the headmaster's harsh facade or the macho facade of the male staff group but I think it's also the result of a grammar school tradition which sees school as the site for teaching and learning and for little else.
>
> *In the secondary modern school* — there is a general ethos among staff that the pastoral care of pupils is an integral part of the teaching role.

This seems to partly be the result of the particular example set over many years by the senior mistress who seems to regard all pupils as members of her family and whose relationship with them seems that of a mother-substitute.

There is no formal pastoral care organization.

Senior mistress (or to a lesser extent HT) concerned with pastoral care of pupils. Senior mistress will visit on her own initiative in cases where she thinks a visit is needed. School and senior staff will also arrange material aid for pupils (clothes etc.) in cases of need. Outside agencies only brought in in 'intractable' cases.

In the comprehensive school — in practice there is no formal pastoral care system in the school. Heads of year and form teachers are argued to carry out pastoral function but there is a distinct lack of enthusiasm about performing any function which does not directly relate to teachers' role as 'Imparter of Knowledge' in the classroom.

Headteacher may — if forced into the position — counsel a pupil and pupil's parents on academic or social matters. Senior mistress (changed two-thirds of the way through the year) carries responsibility for pastoral care of *all* the girls!

Senior staff activity is at a low level and their expressions of concern for the pastoral care of pupils are generally conspicuous by absence.

Head of middle school, on the other hand, seems to have taken a keen interest in non-academic care of pupils in his 'unit'.

When problems become so severe that they cannot be ignored school will, usually, call in outside agencies. If problem relates to truancy, school effort seems to be bent to persuading SS Dept. to go for a prosecution. In general the school attitude to pupils is custodial rather than humane.

Differences between the two systems of education were also in evidence when it came to dealing with particularly difficult or problematic pupils. Such pupils — who were mostly difficult because of continual disciplinary problems but who also included some who were regarded as psychological cases as they had developmental difficulties — were usually dealt with within the schools in the selective system. For the grammar school, contact with the Social Services Department, the Education Welfare Officers, or the Schools Psychological Service of the local education authority was — although known — extremely rare. For the secondary moderns too, contact was rare since they attempted as far as possible to deal with their problems themselves — our notes on one of them record that:

Social Services: Comparatively little contact. The school may liaise with the SS to facilitate material help to the families of pupils but counselling and social control functions are largely carried out within the school.

EWO Service: Sporadic contact when intractable truancy problem occurs but, if needs be, extensive visiting of truant children and their families carried out by school members of staff. EWO involved as a last resort.

Ed Psych Service: Apparent contact only on initiative of the Ed Psych Service. Again learning and behaviour problems contained — seemingly without much thought — in the school. It was a matter of some surprise when as the result of a visitation by the County Ed Psych the school received information that 10 per cent of its pupils could be categorized as ESN. The school had viewed no one as subnormal.

Whereas in the selective system only intractable cases were referred out to specialist agencies, in both the comprehensive schools there was a much greater likelihood of outside agency involvement. In part, this seemed to be a further reflection of the comprehensive's orientation towards academic, rather than social, goals — teachers who were already redefining their role towards the imparting of knowledge and away from the role of developing all aspects of a child's personality seemed likely to carry this progression further and see major problems as simply not their concern. The 'professionalizing' of welfare in the schools as they developed special systems for care and welfare may also have encouraged the same dependence upon professional help from outside the two schools. Also, the two comprehensive's problems with their pupils seemed to have led to a slightly weary fatalism, a low perception of the remediability of pupils' problems and a desire to reduce the amount of emotional investment that teachers were making in a highly stressful school environment.

Whatever the precise reasons for their policy of referring out problem pupils, our field notes on one of the comprehensives tell a very different story to those on the grammar and the secondary modern schools:

Social Services: Quite significant contact, as perhaps one would expect (also contact with Probation).

EWO: After failure of school to get a pupil truant back to school, EWO involved with brief of obtaining a prosecution unless swift resolution of truancy problem effected.

Ed Psych Service: Yes, on a relatively frequent basis.

The similarity between the comprehensive schools and the grammar school in the lack of expressed concern for the pastoral rather than the academic, and the difference between the secondary moderns and the comprehensives in their goals and their organizational arrangements are themes that will recur again and again through this chapter.

School/Parent Relations

In their relations with parents, also, the comprehensive schools took on the grammar school ethos that had been dominant when they had been selective schools and which was still dominant in the selective grammar school. From our knowledge of their functioning before comprehensivization, parental visits to the two grammar schools were very rare, usually concerned with disciplinary matters or academic matters rather than personal problems and usually requested by the schools rather than by the parents.

Consequently, the two schools were not seen by their local communities as anything other than academic institutions with a purely academic, knowledge imparting function. Whilst it is clear that community perceptions of the two comprehensives may well have been influenced by these perceptions of the schools when they were grammar schools, it was apparent to us that the senior management of the two schools themselves perpetuated a view of their parents that saw them both as a potential irritation to the transactions between school and pupil and also as a potential anti-educational influence. Neither school had a parent teacher association in the 1970s. In both communities the parents saw the schools as remote and, needless to say, few parents ever went to the comprehensives with their own problems. Our notes on one of the comprehensives describe this situation:

> One gets the sense that school/parent relations are kept at as formal a level as possible. Parents who wish to discuss problems relating to their children have to make an appointment with the staff member concerned — also a deal of acrimony with one group of parents over county financial support for bus fares. No one member of senior staff appears to take responsibility for PR or liaison with parents — flows, perhaps, from the head's 'isolationism'.

Whilst the comprehensives had minimal commitment to formal links with parents and minimal informal contact (except where teachers and parents met in the one comprehensive that had community used facilities), the selective system was very different in its emphasis. Whilst the grammar school had of course minimal formal and informal contact with parents, the two secondary moderns had much greater commitment. For one of them our notes record that:

> The school has easy, frequent and informal relationships with parents. This contact is two way: parents appear to feel no inhibition in contacting the school to seek help or advice re pupils (or for that matter to make complaints); the school also initiates contact with

parents in the event of serious academic, disciplinary, or pastoral problems. In part, this easy and frequent interaction between the school and parents seems to be facilitated by:

(i) the openness and availability of the headteacher
(ii) the personality and community knowledge of the senior mistress
(iii) the geographical and class similarities of staff and parents

The school functions in part as a social work or relief agency, organizing the provision of clothing etc. for the children of the poorer parents. It is not an unusual occurrence for teachers to teach some pupils dressed in their own families' cast offs. In addition staff members — the senior mistress especially — carry out extensive counselling and containment roles which in many schools would be off-loaded to specialist educational and social work agencies.

Rules, Rewards and Punishments

As we have argued elsewhere (Reynolds and Sullivan, 1979) Treliw schools have usually appeared to use one of two strategies of control of their pupils — incorporation or coercion. Incorporation aims to achieve control through relationships, which are to be attained by blurring status hierarchies, involving pupils in the life of the school and ensuring therapeutic rather than punitive responses to pupil deviance if it occurs. Coercion, by contrast, aims to use external reinforcers of behaviour such as physical punishment, shaming or verbal sanctions in order to motivate pupils to be pro-social in their allegiance to school norms. In the two comprehensives, the strategy of incorporation was simply much more difficult to employ. Size made the development of primary relationships more difficult. The lack of consistency amongst teachers in their rule enforcement and expectations generated a more cynical pupil group. Attempts to incorporate the pupils by incorporating their parents into support of the school were clearly difficult given the attitude of the former grammar school teachers towards parents.

Also — and most importantly — some of the possibilities for incorporation of pupils that the three selective schools used were blocked off from use by the policy decisions made by the comprehensives. Prefect systems were used by all three selective schools as a means of splitting the potentially anti-school pupil sub-culture and as a means of bringing pupils into the organization of the school so that they might share its values — across all three schools, about 30 per cent of the fifth year pupils would have been prefects, a high proportion mostly because of the attempts of the secondary moderns to spread prefectships into the potentially anti-school 'B' streams. In the two comprehensive schools, prefects were drawn only from the sixth forms, and not at all from year 5. A mechanism which in the selective system was encouraging incorporation — even for low stream children — was absent for comparable children in the comprehensive system.

When account is taken of the festivals, the societies, the sports teams, the concerts etc. that existed in all three selective schools, the proportion of pupils' incorporated into pro-school activity would inevitably be higher because of the small size of the schools. At one of the secondary moderns, for example, almost half the entire fifth year that had not some physical disability was in the school soccer team, which had as its travelling band of supporters the others of the year. At either comprehensive school, the proportion of the year involved would have been considerably smaller, particularly since the sixth form pupils tended to fill team places. Also, it is important to note that the lower streams in the comprehensives quite apart from being less likely to participate because of size factors also seemed to participate considerably less than the higher streams. Because of the greater heterogeneity of talent in the two comprehensive schools, there was always a greater chance that a lower ability child would be brought into contact — in the chess club say — with a child of considerably greater ability. This led to lower stream children disassociating themselves from their schools.

The difficulties in the social control of pupils that the comprehensives experienced in the mid 1970s led, as it had done in some of the secondary moderns studied in our earlier work, inevitably towards a tighter organizational regime and towards the increased use of coercion. Whilst the two comprehensives had virtually identical rules to the selective system covering smoking, rudeness, cheek to staff, fighting, jewellery, uniform, chewing gum and the like, the selective system in all three schools had eroded the importance of the rules by not enforcing them strictly, the aim being to ensure that the schools were able to 'hold' their pupils in a relationship with the teaching staff. The comprehensives in the mid-1970s began to enforce their rules more strictly — uniform rules (eroded by years 4 or 5 in the secondary moderns) were applied more strictly, as were rules about not smoking. Levels of corporal punishment began to rise until, in our estimate in 1978, the comprehensive system was beating twice as heavily as the selective system. In one of the comprehensive schools, those beatings were in some cases public, administered in the entrance hall of the school.

We can perhaps illustrate these differences between the two systems in their organizational strategies for pupil control by referring to our field notes on rules and rule enforcement/strictness.

In the smallest secondary modern school, rules that would alienate the pupils were systematically de-emphasized, as our notes on each rule show:

(a) *School Uniform:* A school uniform is specified but there is little if any effort expended in attempting to ensure that it is worn. The school staff feel that it is unrealistic to expect many of their pupils to wear school uniform or many parents to afford it.

(b) *Smoking:* The school has a 'no smoking' rule. Again the rule is seldom acted on. Teachers do not patrol school grounds to catch offenders, nor will they take any action on seeing a pupil smoker unless the smoker is blatant and provocative in his breach of the 'no smoking' rule.

(c) *Rudeness*
(i) *to teachers:* Teachers expect the respect of their pupils but also expect that they have to win it. Respect, however, is not defined as passive subservience. 'Treliw type' aggressive repartee is often a feature of classroom interaction with teacher and pupil engaging in somewhat aggressive and personal wit and sarcasm.
(ii) *to other pupils:* Overall regarded as an area to be resolved by pupils.

(d) *Bullying:* The majority of staff members are insistent that they will, under no circumstances, tolerate the physical or overt psychologicalbullying of one pupil by another — this is, with fighting, one of the few occasions when boys will be referred to the senior master for punishment (corporal) and girls to the senior mistress (for a dressing down).

(e) *Fighting:* As with bullying.

(f) *Swearing:* Swearing at teachers dealt with usually by a severe verbal reprimand or informal physical punishment by teacher involved. Inter-pupil swearing usually ignored unless it is impossible to do so.

(g) *Corporal Punishment:* A very rare occurrence, carried out by Senior Master on boys only for bullying or fighting.

The school philosophy on rule enforcement seems to be a simple one — it doesn't fight battles it knows it cannot win.

The other secondary modern school — although it was stricter in its rule enforcement than the school above — still gave ground or called a 'truce' with its pupils in many areas of school life. Material generated by one of our earlier 'rapport' sessions with fourth year classes before they received their tests from us shows this clearly:

Both 4A and 4B identified as core rules those prohibiting smoking and fighting or bullying. Their definition of core rules were those which they felt that staff were most vigilant in enforcing which meant, for them, those rules which, when infringed were punished by the cane. They listed a whole range of what they believed were lesser rules, i.e., those which carried a lesser punishment or those which were turned a blind eye to. They included in order of importance; running through the school hall (response = telling off), wearing of ear-rings by boys and girls (response = registration of offence and enforcement of removal after the six weeks necessary for the healing of the wound had elapsed), wearing of long hair by boys (response = telling off but apparently no consistent follow up). I was interested in the reaction of the school to wearing of school uniform. It appeared that the school requested the wearing of school uniform and the pupils regarded this as a school rule. However, they explained the fact that perhaps 25 per cent of the boys were not wearing school uniform (over the two forms) by volunteering that the staff did not seem to object as long as the boys wore a tie. Most of the girls were wearing school uniform and said it was expected of them.

The comprehensives, by contrast, had considerably tightened their rule enforcement to cope with their problems in the mid-1970s. Whilst one comprehensive — that with the very poor attendance rate detailed in chapter 4 — seemed to have done this more than the other, the tightening of regime was common to both comprehensives. In the school that moved most towards coercion as a means of control, our notes record the following:

School retained a substantial list of pupil rules:
   no smoking;
   no fighting;
   school uniform (except in sixth or with bottom form 5 streams)
   separate boys' and girls' stairs

There appears to be little or no negotiation about the nature, definition and reasons for school rules between staff and pupils. Staff — and often senior staff — make rules. Pupils are expected to keep them.

Infringement of school rules whether core rules as above or specific rules for specific situations is picked up and quickly dealt with. In cases of continual bad behaviour (i.e., more than one infringement) boy pupils may be sent to male deputy head and punishment in the form of cane across the buttocks will often take place in the entrance of the school with a pupil audience.

(a)   *School Uniform:* School uniform rule which school attempts to enforce without a great deal of success forms I–V. Form VI seem to have exemption from the rule.

(b)   *No Smoking:* No smoking rule is enforced by means of staff patrols to expose smokers. If discovered, smoking is often punished by corporal punishment (boys).

(c)   *Rudeness:* Rudeness to teaching staff is not tolerated and results in referral to deputy headteacher. Again punishable by cane (boys).

(d) *Bullying:* If bullying is detected by a staff member, again referral to deputy headteacher, and again very possible caning.

(e) *Fighting:* Fighting summarily and corporally punished whenever it occurs in the view of a staff member.

(f) *Swearing:* As above.

(g) *Corporal punishment:* Corporal punishment used quite freely in school. Teachers would cuff pupils and formal corporal punishment would be administered by Deputy Head.

Comprehensives and the Elevation of the Academic Organization

It must be clear from our discussion throughout this chapter that the comprehensive system elevated the academic goal of examination attainment to a status that it did not possess in two of the three selective schools. The grammar school of the selective system, of course, was primarily concerned with generating academic rather than social success, as the headteacher indicated in response to our questions:

Question: What do you believe to be the aims and objectives of your school in relation to its pupils?

Answer: I take the traditional division into academic aims and pastoral aims and objectives. I put the academic first. I regard the school as a learning agency and, therefore, most emphasis should be placed on teaching and on the achievement of the highest possible academic standards. Then on the pastoral side I think the school should give the pupils security and identity. It is therefore also a caring institution and in fulfilling this aim links with outside agencies. I think there are limits on the pastoral side to what any school can do and therefore I come back to my basic point that a school is basically a learning agency.

Question: What, for you, are the characteristics of the good school?

Answer: You know the curriculum itself can be an instrument of care. I think if you've got a good curriculum this can be a caring agency because the kids get interested in school. One doesn't achieve this with a proportion of children but one hopes to achieve it with a fair percentage of the children that we get. We get about a 40–50 per cent intake into grammar school, therefore some of our courses are not suitable for a proportion of the pupils who are not up to rigorous academic standards which are set. I suppose it supports what I've answered above. I put high academic standards in first place.

The two secondary moderns, by contrast, put social goals in a much higher position. In the first school, the staff themselves had been questioned by the headteacher using the Musgrove and Taylor (1969) questionnaire on teacher goals — instruction (i.e., the imparting of knowledge) was rated as a third priority, behind moral training (i.e., the inculcation of values and attitudes) and social training (i.e., encouraging politeness). The headteacher himself gave academic and social goals an equal importance and went on to say:

> I think that most teachers — and I agree with this — see care of their children to be an integral part of their job. After all, pupils are people with problems and aspirations and — especially with the sort of pupils we've got — the teacher learns to cater for all aspects of the individual pupil's needs. We are a bit like caretaker parents — sometimes strict when we have to be but I like to think we are caring.

The headteacher in some of his own writing on the secondary modern school tradition quoted with approval an author who had argued that:

> The modern school cannot pretend to send into the world pupils with much book learning in the accepted sense, but the best schools certainly help boys and girls to enter the world with sufficient poise and confidence to face their immediate future with enthusiasm and desire to learn. (Violet Gordon).

In the other school, the headteacher explicitly downgraded academic goals:

> We don't have very high academic aims — objectives linked to that are really concerned with maximising what the kids have got whatever that might be.
>
> One aim is to find out therefore what the kids' aptitudes are. Some of them might be slightly inclined to be academic but we can't call them academic in a blanket way as in grammar school, so here there is an individualized search for aptitudes so that you get a bundle of smaller groups rather than a larger group that you peg as academic. We don't peg them as non-academic either — open minded about it. The primary aim is to satisfy kid's spectrum of aptitudes.
>
> Objectives: (i) decide on some pattern of evaluation so that we can make a search
>
> (ii) evaluate objectively/subjectively — ask a teacher's opinion so that what a teacher says is given more weight than what some odd test says, although we don't ignore objective results
>
> We fly more by the seat of your pants in a place like this because you are dealing with personalities.

In reply to a question on what makes the good school, he argued that:

> In a school like this — a close neighbourhood school because not
> being a selective school obviously we're not going to have a wide
> catchment area — we're going to have then to some extent a lot
> of our concerns are going to be strictly local, so what is a good
> school related partly to those local requirements. I would say —
> characteristics of a good school — it relates closely to its own
> particular catchment area, relates requirements of that catchment area
> to general requirements of schooling and tries to make a good
> marriage between the two. That's talking in general aims. Teachers
> and pupils will have characteristics which will make or break a
> school regardless of its aims. Characteristics of a good school are:
> relationship of respect between staff and pupils as a whole; good
> relations between individual pupils and individual staff. Can get odd
> teacher who is not able to promote good individual relations but can
> be protected by a good general relationship. Mutual respect is some-
> thing that can occur. What promotes this respectful relationship
> generally is a guideline given to head in terms of his personal rela-
> tionship with his staff and with his pupils and in what he conveys to
> staff and pupils.

In response to a question about the importance of the teacher performing a
pastoral role, the same headteacher argued that:

> It's a value loaded question! But there's a temptation today that if
> you've got a problem you set up an organization. Very often you
> just create more problems. I think the essential relationship in educa-
> tion is finally between the teacher and the pupil and I've seen this. It
> is a fact that you can have a great system and the teacher in front of
> his class has still got his own problems and that's his own world and
> he must relate to the children in some kind of way, for many
> teachers it's a very useful way to relate to them pastorally so that he
> takes a personal interest in them. I think that this is productive in
> terms of the teaching process. In that he sets up a situation where the
> kid thinks he cares about him and the kid is more apt to listen to
> what he says. More apt to adopt him as a model for one thing and to
> come back to the other point: Kids will not take much notice of an
> example unless they've got some sort of respect and a feeling of
> being personally involved with the teacher. I reject any idea that the
> teacher can be simply an instructor. He can in certain areas — there
> are very objective children — we call them academic children who
> are able to function in an objective, impersonal way and regard the
> teacher as a role not a person. There are far more children who need
> a personal relationship — a human basis to their learning situation.

By comparison with the two secondary modern schools, it was the academic side of education which the two comprehensives emphasized, making them similar to the grammar school of the selective system. In response to a question asking him to describe the school's goals, one headteacher listed them in order as follows:

(a) To maintain and improve academic standards for the ablest.
(b) To encourage the less able and provide them with qualifications for a scenario with 2.5 m unemployed.
(c) To provide the best possible conditions for staff and pupils to do their work.
(d) To encourage the virtues of honesty, sincerity, hard work, originality and consideration for others.

The academic goals of the other headteacher of the comprehensive system were clearly spelt out in his letter to prospective parents — again, the academic advantages of comprehensivization are mentioned, together with the theme of spreading the grammar school tradition to cover new areas of the pupil ability range:

> ... if a child has ability and is prepared to work he has as much chance of achieving good examination results as in the old grammar school situation. Indeed, since the new comprehensive schools are more generously staffed we can do more with regard to the number of subjects taken. Additionally, children who would have gone to modern schools did only the leavers examination. Some children would be transferred to the grammar school and a tiny handful on two occasions did some 'O' levels from a modern school. CSE work was not done in the modern schools before we went comprehensive.
>
> All the 'O' level subject groups of grammar school days have been maintained in the curriculum. 'O' level woodwork is being done as well as engineering theory and workshop practice (both were not done at the same time in grammar school days). The same is true of dress and design and home economics. 'O' level geology has been added. In art, biology, mathematics and geography the combined syllabus is followed. This means that children do one examination in these subjects. If they do well they get an 'O' level grade. If they fail to attain this they do not get nothing, but may be awarded a CSE grade. 'O' level physical science is tried from form 4 by the most able science pupils.
>
> The children who would have been weak in a grammar school and those who would have before gone to a modern school are now able to try a very wide range of CSE subjects — physics, chemistry, biology, human biology, general science, motor mechanics, metalwork, woodwork, technical drawing, needlework, home economics, office practice, commerce, consumer economics, typing, history,

geography, scripture, music, French studies, Welsh studies and art in addition to the basic CSE English literature introduced recently.

For children who go on to form 6, in addition to all the old grammar school 'A' levels (except for zoology and botany for which 'A' level biology has been substituted) there are extra 'O' levels not done in grammar school days — British constitution, classical studies, economic history and law.

We believe in hard work and homework.

Together with the de-emphasis of the social by comparison with the academic in the comprehensives were three other changes that merely served to increase pupil problems. Firstly, an increased academic emphasis led to much greater emphasis upon competition between pupils in the comprehensives, both of which utilized annual examinations, termly reports and grading systems for pieces of work and for individual subjects. Secondly, homework was used in both comprehensive schools not just for the higher ability bands but for those in the middle ability band also, involving those pupils in between an hour and an hour-and-a-half's work each night if they attempted it. Thirdly, in order to ensure that the examination bands (the top three streams in each school) were actually containing the most able pupils so that examination success for them and for the school would ensue, both schools adopted a policy of quite frequent promotion and demotion. In the one comprehensive where we collected information on this, approximately ten children went 'up' into and ten 'down' from the top band each year, after the school examinations. Out of a year of just over 200 in this school, then, perhaps sixty would have changed bands over the first three years that they spent in school, since bands solidified after the end of year 3 with the approach of public examination related courses.

In the secondary modern schools, none of the above three factors were operative. There was, firstly, very little competition at all between pupils — the headteacher of one argued '. . . it is my impression that we encourage each pupil to reach the best rather than pit one against the other', whilst the other said:

Competition depends upon how many losers you've got and I've got an awful lot of losers. Competition is bad for losers. I try to avoid competition. I try to get them to work together towards a common aim. I try to avoid competition but if a lad is particularly distinguished we try to give them full recognition but as one of our boys.

There was, secondly, no homework regularly set, although in both schools staff used to stay on at school after the end of lessons to help prepare candidates for the examinations about six weeks before they were due. Thirdly, the pupil groups were remarkably stable over time — only 10 per cent of pupils, if that, were likely to be moved between forms in the first three years of schooling.

The effect of these different approaches to the world of the academic in the two systems is easy to predict. Many of the comprehensive pupils resented their homework, regarding it as interfering with their social life and increasingly refused to do it by year 4. The competition, whilst it may have done something to improve the self-image of those who won it, did little to improve the commitment or morale of those in the ranks of the losers. The mobility between streams generated a further fragmented, less cohesive pupil group which was changing in composition over time. The social engineering of ambition or spreading of academic goals through the middle third of the ability range that the comprehensives were trying generated, if we are correct, a more alienated, resentful and in some senses split and anomic pupil group by comparison with the non-academic secondary moderns.

It would be wrong for us to conclude this analysis of school processes without stressing a number of important points. Firstly, it will be clear from our discussion here that the two schools that we have jointly analyzed as 'the comprehensive system' were not completely similar in their ethos or organizational arrangements. There were small differences in personnel, in ideology and in the usual range of idiosyncratic factors which combine to generate a school ethos or organizational tone.

In spite of this, though, and in spite of the fact that we have clearly lost explanatory variance because we have not analyzed all five schools on an individual basis, we have analyzed the five schools on the basis of 'system against system' because we simply consider the component schools of each system to have considerably more in common than they have not in common. Furthermore, this study is part of an ongoing strategy with three component parts which has aimed to test which school factors appear to be associated with school effectiveness and performance. Part one was a comparison of eight schools *within* the selective system (Reynolds *et al*, 1987), study two is this system *against* system work and study three is a comparison of two differentially effective schools *within* the comprehensive system. To make this present study of *system* effectiveness instead into a study of *school* effectiveness would have been to destroy the integrity of the overall research design.

Secondly, we must report that the two systems were similar when compared together on a number of other process factors which existing school effectiveness research has identified as being important in affecting pupil outcomes. Liaison with feeder primary schools seemed to be pursued equally by both systems, with quite elaborate systems of visits by teachers to feeder schools prior to transfer and with identical information being passed by the feeder schools to the secondary schools concerned. Within-lesson activity time also seemed to be utilized to a very similar extent in the two systems — traditionality was the rule in the separation of subjects, the role of the teacher as knowledge distributor, the highly passive pupil role, and the very limited use made of audio visual aids, work packs and any other form of 'new' method of distributing knowledge. Pupils working together in groups was infrequently seen in either system, save in the remedial departments of the two comprehensives and the bottom streams of the secondary moderns. Most of the lessons we observed consisted of 60–70 per cent of the time being spent in teacher 'talk and chalk' about the subject concerned, which itself was usually followed by pupils doing exercises or written work for the remainder of the double lesson blocks. Whilst by year 4 there were some hints that the lower streams in the comprehensives were being badly affected by pupil absence having effects on the teacher effort that was being put into lesson preparation and school activity generally, the quality of classroom experience consumed by individual pupils was remarkably similar across the two systems.

Other areas of school life marked by system similarity were the use of school trips, whether the headteacher taught (all did between four and six lessons a week) and some teacher biographical factors (sex distribution, age distribution, whether they lived inside or outside the community and take up of in-service education).

Thirdly, it is also important for us to note that some of the internal school processes that we described in this chapter may have resulted from the large size of the comprehensive schools rather than from their comprehensiveness. A move towards more routinized or bureaucratized pastoral care systems, some moves towards greater pupil coercion, some of the fragmentation of the institutions and some of the problems that the headteachers of these schools faced in their administration may reflect on the schools' large size, although other British research evidence has not suggested size of school to be an important factor in affecting outcomes (see reviews in Rutter, 1983; and Reynolds, 1982b). Although this may be a possible explanation for some of the comprehensive schools' internal processes and poor overall performance, in our view most of those internal processes resulted from factors (like a commitment to academic standards, the grammar school tradition or the expectations held of the schools by their communities) that were completely independent from any size factor. Simply, we believe from our knowledge that it is the comprehensiveness of our schools more than their size which explains the findings we have reported here.

Conclusions

In general, then, it must be clear that our two comprehensives were in many ways similar to the grammar schools whose traditions they had been locally and nationally expected to extend. Overall, the two comprehensives had a grammar school orientation. Both heads were former grammar school headteachers, two thirds of department heads were from the grammar schools and both schools concentrated much effort on their sixth forms — in one of the comprehensives, the sixteen heads of department gave on average over twenty lessons a week to the sixth form. The teaching staff were streamed —

the former grammar school teachers and a few of the secondary moderns' more experienced staff taught the top bands, graduate secondary modern teachers and some grammar school teachers the middle bands, and the new, inexperienced or 'burnt out' secondary modern teachers taught the lower bands. The schools adopted a grammar school distance in their attitudes to parents, adopted a grammar school concentration on the academic rather than the pastoral, kept grammar school rules that had been eroded in the secondary moderns, and had a grammar school orientation towards the use of pupil/pupil competition as a motivator.

In their use of curriculum, too, the comprehensives were highly traditional institutions. Whereas the selective system had none of the CSE Mode Three schemes that have been seen by many as permitting a redefinition of curricular content towards more 'relevant' knowledge, the two comprehensives only developed three such schemes between them — these three schemes only actually affected a very insignificant proportion of their pupils since they were in the subjects of consumer economics, archaeology and child care. Whilst the comprehensives were able to offer more practical subjects as we have noted earlier, the curricular *content* of the conventional range of subjects in the sciences and in the humanities was virtually indistinguishable from that of the selective system, a hardly surprising finding since both systems were tied to the same curriculum for their examination children since both used the examination system of the Welsh Joint Education Committee.

In only one area of school life — the ability grouping system — did the comprehensive sector move in the radical direction or touch the 'egalitarian' model of comprehensiveness (Marsden, 1971) that many supporters of the schools would have wanted. Whilst the three selective schools all continued to stream by ability for all five years of normal school life (even though the streams were not labelled 'A' and 'B' in the two modern schools), one comprehensive went completely mixed ability in the first year followed by a banding system in years 2 and 3 and an option choice system involving setting in years 4 and 5. The other comprehensive banded into two broad ability bands for the first three years (with a remedial group separately), which followed the same broad curriculum except for some substitution of extra English language instead of a foreign language in years 2 and 3 for the lower band. Both schools argued that their forms were mixed ability within a band, although there was some evidence that this may not have been wholly the case. Both schools had made the change from rigid streaming to mixed ability or to banding explicitly hoping that the attitudes and abilities of the bottom two-thirds and especially the bottom third of the ability range would benefit from the change.

Whether this was of benefit to these pupils but was swamped in its impact by other factors is unclear. All that is clear is that for a variety of reasons, the comprehensive schools during the period of our studies come close to the bilateral forms of schooling that some (Benn and Simon, 1970) have argued to be an intermediate stage between selective and 'true' compre-hensive schools. Both comprehensive schools continued, in fact, to see pupils as either grammar *or* secondary modern pupils for a number of years — one of the headteachers in a letter to the Director of Education about sixth-form staying on rates talked of comparisons with the old days being difficult 'because nowadays more top band (i.e. grammar school) pupils are doing more CSEs than before we went comprehensive and nowadays modern secondary pupils in the comprehensive school are sitting CSE papers ...'. The selective school ethos was clearly living on.

Part Three: Conclusions and Recommendations

Chapter 6

Towards Policies for Effective Comprehensive Schooling

The comprehensive school ...... took shape not from a clear educational vision but from a political solution to the problem of pupil selection.
(Maurice Holt)

I think the great mistake we made was in assuming the academic horse would pull the social cart.
(Treliw teacher)

For those concerned with secondary education, the data we have presented on the problems and poor performance of our two comprehensive schools by comparison with the selective system must have made somewhat depressing reading. Education has always been the great hope of social reformers (Reynolds and Jones, 1978). Comprehensive schooling in particular was a reform in which large numbers of people vested their emotional and political energy.

In this concluding chapter we want to try and attempt to suggest ways in which comprehensive schooling can be made more effective so that the schools might begin to attain the goals that have been posited for them by reformers. We do not conclude from our studies in Treliw that education cannot compensate for society or that educational reform can have no effects on the wider society. Indeed, it is clear (Reynolds, 1985a) that schools do have major effects upon pupils and that educational reform experiments — if they learn from the failure of previous models that have crashed! — can have positive effects. Those positive effects and how to attain them will be outlined after we have summarized our evidence and our analyses.

The Argument Reviewed

Our earlier chapters developed a thesis that comprehensive schools were developed as a result of a number of pressures. Whilst they do not seem to have been part of any egalitarian conspiracy to socially engineer the erosion of capitalism as portrayed by some right-wing commentators, it seems likely that their rapid growth owes something to a variety of factors: (i) to changing conceptions of social justice in British society; (ii) to research evidence showing the ineffectiveness of the selective system; and (iii) to the interests of labour (in hopefully having more talent to sell) and capital (in hopefully having more talent to employ). Whilst all these factors predisposed change towards comprehensivization, the political factor of the Labour party's commitment to the schools was what precipitated their rapid growth. Seeing that the system of selection at 11 was both unpopular and discredited, yet knowing that the grammar schools had status and respect amongst all sectors of the community, there were clear electoral advantages for the Labour party to be gained from embracing a notion of the comprehensive school as a grammar school for all, extending the old grammar ethos to new sections of the ability range. Crucially, the internal organization of the school was left unspecified, so that various groups within the left and other groups outside could still be in favour of comprehensives, even while wanting different types of school in terms of internal organization.

We went on to look at the research evidence as to whether the schools have attained the academic and social goals that were posited for them — the development of *more* talent, the fairer *distribution of talent* across social groups and the breakdown of differences in social attitudes/social stratification in favour of *more communality*. Although there is not a great quantity of evidence to look at and although the methodological quality of much of that evidence is pitifully poor, in general it would seem that comprehensives have failed to attain any of the goals that social reformers have set for them. Some recent studies — more methodologically sound — give hints that whilst the comprehensives may have held or even outperformed the academic success rates of the selective system, on more social outcomes the schools may be doing less well than the selective system. Other recent work shows the schools failing academically also.

Our own research to see if comprehensives are more or less effective than the selective system suffers, of course, from a number of disadvantages. It is mostly on boys, with slightly restricted information on individuals, based in an atypical, disadvantaged, white, Welsh community with an above average proportion of grammar school places. Our comprehensives were also relatively new schools. However, in all other respects we have been uniquely fortunate — whilst we are not reporting the results of a true experiment with random allocation of individuals to the different systems, we are a research study based on an experiment of nature where two virtually identical communities received different educational institutions simply because of the arrangement of their stock of school buildings. We are of cohort design, with comprehensives taking the full ability range, from defined catchment areas, and with information on the intakes, outcomes and processes of all our schools. By contrast to the research effort on this issue, we are able to offer definitive answers to some of the questions that other researchers have been unable to answer.

Our data showed the two systems of education as having very similar pupils at intake, judged by individual data on ability and personality. After statistically controlling for the effects of these differences on our outcome measures, the selective system slightly out-performed the comprehensive system on academic output, and considerably out-performed the system on one of the attitude to school scales and on the locus of control scale.

On delinquency and attendance, the selective system again performed considerably better, a performance that could not be explained by our group data on social conditions in the catchment areas of the schools. Looking at which part of the ability range seems to account for this ineffective comprehensive performance suggests that overall it is the middle of the ability range that does worse in the comprehensives on the individual data. On group data, it is the bottom two-thirds of the ability range that does worst on delinquency and the bottom third of the ability range that does worse on attendance in the comprehensives. Again it must be said that the differences between the results of the different ability ranges are small on the academic outcome measure but considerably larger on the social measures we have utilised.

The Comprehensive's Failures

Our understanding of within-school processes was subsequently used to try to understand why the comprehensives were such ineffective institutions for lower ability pupils and for the attainment of the social rather than the academic outcomes of schooling. The schools had trouble settling and were confused about the goals of the new institutions — although the system had certain resource advantages, it also had management difficulties and a resulting lack of cohesion and consistency in staff response to pupil needs. Pastoral care became bureaucratized in the schools and the academic and pastoral sides increasingly split. School parent relations were less close and the pupil control orientation of the system — somewhat inevitably given the lack of pupil involvement — became more coercive than the selective system. Overall, the academic goals of education were emphasized more than the social goals that both the secondary modern schools had laid great stress on for their lower ability pupils, and overall the comprehensive system appeared to be much closer to the orientation and ethos of the grammar school tradition than it was to that of the secondary moderns. Whilst the comprehensive system had modified the pupil ability grouping system in an attempt to help the development of lower ability pupils, in all other areas of school life including that of the curriculum the two schools were notable for their conventionality. As schools, the comprehensives had not managed to reach the accommodations with pupils reached in the secondary moderns and consequently as grammar schools for all, they were unable to hold or socially control those pupils for whom the grammar school and its academic traditions were a notable irrelevance.

The processes that account for the schools' social failure and their failure with the bottom portion of the ability range seemed to involve the progressive disassociation of those pupils from their schools from the middle of year 3. The academic emphasis, pressure and ethos had generated a counter-reaction from amongst those lower ability pupils. The fragmentation and lack of cohesion amongst the staff and the associated inconsistent use of sanctions and punishments alienated the same pupils. Bureaucratized pastoral care often seemed more concerned with control than with care. Little parental pressure to conform was in evidence, since the comprehensive schools did not attempt to incorporate the parents of their lower ability pupils. The schools' attempts to ensure the social control of their pupils by tightening rule enforcement and by enforcing key rules more strictly simply generated further alienation. A cycle of mutually reinforcing events was set up which progressively generated more alienated pupils, a more hostile staff response, further pupil misbehaviour and disassociation from the life of the schools and yet further adverse teacher perceptions and withdrawal of emotional investment from their pupils. From this analysis, it is perhaps easy to understand how the comprehensive school pupils did so poorly on the locus of control scales that measured the extent to which they felt that they could influence the world around them or were in charge of their own lives. Simply, these pupils did not in any sense 'own' the institution that was educating them.

In all their attempts to combat their problems, many of which had been anticipated by those senior staff who had begun running the schools in the mid 1970s, the comprehensives had hoped that the instrumental attractions of improved practical courses, access to former grammar school teachers and the prospects of getting into the former grammar school streams and thereby being entered for 'O' levels would prove the necessary carrot to ensure pupil cooperation and tolerance. We had much impressionistic evidence that the practical subjects were popular with the bottom two-thirds of the ability range and many of these pupils actually chose their days to attend school on the basis of whether or not subjects like metalwork, woodwork, bricklaying and motor mechanics were actually on the timetable. We also have evidence that the comprehensives actually did enter more of their pupils for high status examinations than did the selective schools. Only forty-six out of 101 pupils from the selective system (the grammar streams plus a handful from the former secondary moderns) were actually entered for 'O' levels in year 5; in the comprehensive system, the figure was 123 out of 227. All our evidence is, though, that the expressive failure of the schools to develop good relationships with their pupils was not outweighed in effects by their attempts to instrumentally tie their pupils into supporting their schools. The academic horse was simply unable to pull the social cart.

Effective Secondary Modern Schooling

The processes at work in the two comprehensive schools that generated major social problems amongst the bottom two-thirds of the ability range stand in stark contrast to the situation in the two secondary modern schools. They, like the majority of the secondary modern schools in Treliw that we have described in detail elsewhere (Reynolds and Sullivan, 1979), used what we have called the incorporative strategy of controlling their pupils and mobilising them to accept and support school goals and adult society goals.

The major components of this strategy were two-fold; the incorporation of pupils into the organization of the school and the incorporation of their parents into support of the school. Pupils were incorporated within the classroom by encouraging them to take an active and participative role in lessons and by letting them intervene verbally without the teacher's explicit directions. Pupils were also far more likely to be allowed and encouraged to work in groups. Outside formal lesson time, attempts were made to incorporate pupils into the life of the school by utilising other strategies. One of these was the use of numbers of pupil prefects and monitors, taken from all parts of the school ability range, whose role was largely one of supervision of other pupils in the absence of staff members. Such a practice appeared to have had the effects of inhibiting the growth of anti-school pupil sub-cultures because of its effects in creating senior pupils who were generally supportive of the schools. It also had the latent and symbolic function of providing pupils with a sense of having some control over their within-school lives; that this degree of control was offered under conditions which revealed the manifest nature of the schools' internal power relationships is also true, however, because the removal of these symbols gave the school a further sanction it could utilize against its possible deviants.

Another means of incorporation into the values and norms of the school was the development of *inter*personal rather than *im*personal relationships between teachers and pupils. Basically, teachers in these two incorporative modern schools attempted to tie pupils into the value systems of the school and of the adult society by means of developing good personal relationships with them. In effect, the judgment was being made in these schools that internalization of teacher values was more likely to occur if pupils saw teachers as 'significant others' deserving of respect. Good relationships were consequent upon minimal use of overt institutional control (so that pupil behaviour was relatively unconstrained), low rates of physical punishment, a tolerance of a limited amount of 'acting out' (such as by smoking or gum chewing for example), a pragmatic hesitancy to enforce rules which may have provoked rebellion and an attempt to reward good behaviour rather than punish bad behaviour. Within this school ethos, instances of pupil deviance evoked therapeutic, rather than coercive, responses from within the school. Attempts to incorporate pupils were closely parallelled by attempts to enlist the support of their parents by the establishment of close, informal or semi-formal relations between teachers and parents, the encouraging of informal visits by parents to the school and the frequent and full provision of information to parents that concerned pupil progress and staff decisions.

It seems to us that these secondary modern schools succeeded as agencies of social control because they offered a relatively pleasant environment, characterised by the staff's avoidance of conflict with a group of children who, on the whole, were not dependent upon the rewards of the school for their future livelihoods (Reynolds, 1975). Generally, the secondary modern school pupils had low social aspirations and their schools recognized that, unlike the grammar schools, they were unable to offer the 'carrot' of future occupational success in return for an instrumental compliance with school norms. In these schools order, social control and the internalization of adult standards was ensured by the use of the interpersonal controls that are consequent upon good personal relationships.

If one remembers, with Emile Durkheim, that the basic role of the school is one of initiation into both the specific and general values of adult society, then the secondary moderns were succeeding because the initiation that they offered these children was a relatively pleasurable experience, unlike that offered in the comprehensives to children of similar ability.

Our smallest secondary modern school illustrates the incorporative approach in action. Truces existed on all major rules, with low levels of physical punishment and a counselling rather than punishment orientated approach to dealing with rule breaking. On only one occasion did we ever see any form of physical coercion used and that was when a highly disturbed child had to be physically restrained from smashing up the school classrooms. Relationships between teachers and pupils were close and seen as necessary to ensure an adequate power for the school as a mechanism of socialisation. The joking relationship noticed frequently by school ethnographers (Woods, 1983) often featured in informal interaction within the school.

The headteacher devolved considerable power to individual staff members, including virtually all save the most serious disciplinary matters. Given the relatively well experienced nature of the staff, curriculum matters too were virtually completely devolved. Pastoral matters that were unable to be handled by the form teachers were dealt with by the deputy or the headteacher. Relations between headteacher and staff were mostly cordial, with little of the friction we observed in the comprehensive schools. Headteacher and staff would spend break times together and would even meet socially in each others houses. Teacher/teacher relations were generally marked by harmony, partly because of the absence of cliques or sub groups. Low levels of staff turnover produced a stable set of social relationships; cohesion and a consistency of expectations were the hallmark of the staff culture. Rules were therefore likely to be enforced similarly by different staff members, leading to a consistency of pupil expectations of the school regime.

As far as possible, the school was reward orientated rather than punishment orientated. In the classrooms, through the use of sports teams, the use of prefects and in many other ways in the life of the school, the aim was to motivate pupils by praise for their good or pro-social behaviour rather than by punishment for their bad or anti-social behaviour. Punishments, if used, were given always at an individual rather than at a group level.

Overall, the teaching staff held quite favourable perceptions of the surrounding community and its population. Although economically it was regarded as disadvantaged, it was also seen as having a viable and vibrant culture in the form of its choirs, bands and societies. Furthermore, the survival of extensive community and family ties that were in general supportive of conventional social values ensured that in the staff's view there was an organized defence of pro-social conduct in the shape of the community. Linking with the parents of this community was an integral part of the school's mission.

The flavour of pupils' life at the school is perhaps best illustrated by this description of school life by one of the fourth year pupils:

> The understanding of teachers at this school is fair, and most teachers are kind and thoughtful to pupils, but not at most schools, where you can't talk to a teacher, but here, if you have a problem at any time you can go to the teachers with it. I'd like to think that all schools are like ours, but I guess that's impossible. Most people think that our school is a dump, but not the children who work here. When something goes wrong in this school we try to stick up for it, but very often we are put down by other people, who don't know us very well. If one of the teachers was taken ill and we had been pulling his or her leg before this happened I am sure that we, the pupils, would help our teacher get well. In other words, our school is like one big happy family to all the boys and girls here. Some people say that they wouldn't like their boy or girl to come to this school but when they see and talk to our teachers then they know that this school is just right for their children. I know for a fact that I am glad I came to this school and not to . . .

The school's headteacher described his school and his community in equally positive terms:

> In spite of the inadequacies of the environment as regards social amenities and employment, the children seem on the whole to like living in the area and would not wish to move elsewhere. Although the vast majority of houses are of the terraced type, and are very old, the majority nowadays are owner occupied, and the owners express their pride by keeping them brightly painted and in good repair. Apart from the minority of children, the pupils have a comfortable home.
>
> The environment does not seem to have adverse effects upon the

pupils. Neither does the old building seem to constrain the pupils and teachers to any large extent, and is well compensated for by the good pupil teacher relationships that seem to apply in the school.

Inter-staff relationships are very good, and the staff is a particularly stable one. This is obviously helped by the generous 'points' allocation to the school, which allows nearly every teacher to be on a salary of scale II or above. As can be seen from the teachers' answers to the questionnaire, very few would like to change schools, being content to remain as they are.

The valley, being more or less a one class society, with the teachers coming from the same social background as the children, also helps student staff relationships, as the teachers fully understand the social background of the pupils. The older members of the teaching staff also have a close contact with the community, knowing personally the mothers, fathers and relations of the pupils. This is particularly useful in the case of the deputy headteacher, in her pastoral role in the school, and in her relationships with parents.

Inter-school relationships are good. There is close liaison with the contributing primary schools, and also with the secondary schools associated in the area with this school. This should make integration an easier task when the school eventually becomes part of a comprehensive.

Secondary modern schools, the results of the 1944 Education Act, have been in existence for thirty years. What of their future? Throughout the country, secondary modern schools are being phased out in favour of comprehensive schools. The plans are that the school should become part of a comprehensive school in 1978. Thus the school will be one of the last in this area of the tripartite system begun in 1944.

When this happens, I hope that there will be full consultation between all the schools involved, so that we may not lose the benefits of good student staff relationships built up over the years in a small school. It is up to the teachers and myself to see that we do everything in our power to make it a smooth transition for the children in our charge.

This secondary modern school's emphasis upon social rather than academic goals for its less able pupils is best illustrated by quoting at some length the views of the deputy head, who saw herself more as a parent than as a mere inculcator of academic qualifications:

Let me say from the start that the teacher's function is to educate, to help, to guide, to be a mature friend to the child. This does not mean that he or she is to regard the child as being an equal. If the child is undisciplined, perverse, anti-social then the teacher cannot allow him to go his own way any more than the parent can allow him to do so without affecting his whole future. It is our duty to be firm, reliable in our guidance and children appreciate our strength in doing so. But it is important to show the child why we do this to prove to him or her that it is just because we are concerned that we are taking a firm line. Children appreciate our consistency, our reliability when this is coupled with understanding. We must question their actions and get them to think through the consequences of their actions and in doing so we help them to think for themselves, to be more confident and happier in what they do and their relationships with others.

I therefore do not believe that there are barriers between teachers and pupils. There is no need to preserve a mystique. What we want is for us to understand them and for them to understand us. It is a matter of good personal relationships. These are all important. Pupils are all different and they all have different problems. We want them aired and we must regard them with sympathy. This is not a public thing. It is possible of course to practise a degree of mass counselling in class or assembly and to have group discussion. Children who respond to this are not in general those who are the problem children. For these there is no alternative to individual guidance and to a confidential talk. You must give them your time and they will appreciate this. You must express concern and even involve yourself in what happens to them outside school, even within their own families. Many times I have invited parents to the school and on most of these occasions the parent, like the child, adopts a hostile attitude towards the school until I explain my position — that I am there to help and that I am in a sense representing the child just as the parent is. I point out that if the parent pulls against us then he or she is likely to win, but the child will be the loser and will fall prey of some other potent but less reliable influence, like a delinquent peer group. In almost every case I have met with co-operation before the end of the interview. Reason and kindness are always disarming.

It is perhaps symbolic of the neglected, and often misunderstood, traditions of secondary modern schooling that only this school out of five had a suggestion box for the pupils to write in with their choice of end-of-term activities.

Are Our Schools Typical?

We are completely satisfied that the results and the relative performance of the two systems of education that we have reported here accurately reflect the situation in our research community in the late 1970s. What we cannot be sure of is the extent to which our results and the explanations which account for them, would be reproduced in other communities in Great Britain.

We have mentioned before the atypicality of Wales' educational history and the atypicality of its educational performance currently. The schools appear more conventional, traditional and conservative by comparison with those of England for example. The comprehensives of Wales spend slightly more per pupil than those of England, although this does not seem translated into higher per pupil expenditure at the 'chalk-face' (Reynolds, 1982a and 1983). Our comprehensive schools were new, without the time to settle and to generate a consistent organizational style that other schools in other areas might have had.

Nevertheless, these are problems which any educational research faces, since the variety of organizational styles and curricular content within the comprehensive sector is large. There is variation in the curriculum so large that talk of any common curriculum is misleading (Morgan, 1980). There is variation between comprehensive schools in the length of the school day (Hilsom and Cane, 1971) and in the allocation of time to different subjects (Wilcox, 1985). There is substantial variation between schools in their ethos (Rutter, 1979) and in their organizational styles as revealed in Inspectorate reports. The typical or common comprehensive school is likely, therefore, to be a difficult creature to find and therefore all we can do here is simply present the implications of our work for *all* comprehensive schools even though our work is based only on *some* comprehensive schools.

In spite of the possible atypicality of our comprehensives by comparison with the national pattern, it is interesting and reassuring to us that many other commentators and researchers have recently begun to report on comprehensive schools that look very similar in their regimes to ours. Ball's (1985) study of the emergence of a comprehensive system from the amalgamation of selective schools portrays a rather similar 'grammar school take over' of the management of the new system. D. Hargreaves' (1982) challenging outline of possible reforms in comprehensive schooling lists as a major problem 'the dominant emphasis given to the cognitive intellectual domain in the schools' and portrays much of the same continuing grammar school curriculum and organizational style as we do here. Dingle (1984) writes about his own successful comprehensive school and the *able* children. Weeks' (1986) recent study of London comprehensives shows them facing very similar social problems to our schools in Treliw, although these other schools have clearly moved much more quickly than our comprehensives in attempting to solve them. Riseborough (1981) looked at how a group of former secondary modern teachers found themselves passed over when graduates with academic rather than social goals began to dominate the new comprehensives.

In these recent studies, the comprehensive schools they portray and study appear to be very like the ones that we have researched in Treliw. If our schools are argued to be atypical, then simply we join the company of a fair number of other educational researchers.

Changing the Schools

Looking back at the decade during which comprehensive schools have arrived in our research community, it is the inevitability of their failure that most saddens us. There was nationally no specification of the forms of organization that were to be utilized within the schools and no clear commitment to any specifically comprehensive practice or curricular content. Indeed, given the relative autonomy of the British educational system from any central control (Reynolds, 1984a), it is hard to see that any central commitment would have necessarily influenced local practice in any direct way. There was no reason for central government to legislate for the content of comprehensive schools since it had no power to determine school organization or style.

There was nationally no clear statement of comprehensives' goals, except for the relatively unspecific commitment to the goals of improving the quantity of academic talent and the redistribution of it through the social class structure that occasionally appeared in speeches from politicians and educationists. In the absence of political commitment to social, rather than academic, goals and to the development of lower, rather than higher, ability pupils, what Marsden (1971) calls the 'market model' of the school has predominated. Parental pressure generated instrumentally oriented institutions — policy initiatives in the late 1970s, such as the publication of schools' examination results, have merely intensified such pressures on the schools. The popularity and high status of the grammar schools made their imitation by the new comprehensive schools highly likely. The public dislike of 'one-off' selection procedures at 11 and of the secondary modern school form of secondary education made comprehensive education as 'grammar schools for all' an attractive political proposition.

So inevitable were the processes that we have described that many educationists within our community actually foresaw many of the problems that the first generation of comprehensive schooling would bring. The staff of one of our secondary modern schools — when asked by the headteacher in a questionnaire — replied that 70 per cent were 'undesirous' or 'very undesirous' of the school becoming comprehensive. The high figure of 77 per cent thought they would not be happier in a comprehensive situation. Whilst the headteacher publicly stated to us that '... we will not lose the good staff/pupil relationship when we do become a comprehensive school', privately many of his staff and he himself feared for what comprehensivization would mean for they themselves and for their lower ability children.

The resulting uneasy marriage of different traditions and the split between the classes taught by former modern school and former grammar school colleagues can be seen as a way whereby potentially insecure teaching groups attempted to maintain a professional role that they were secure with, in a comprehensive situation where they were insecure.

Inevitably then — and foreseen by many — comprehensive schools in our community had major problems of goal direction and of organization. Policies about the schools locally and policies about them nationally have always been *reactive*, not *purposive*, as the institutions have fought to cope with their historical legacy and with the demands made on them to maximize their educational outcomes within budgets that have remained substantially unchanged. What must be done then to ensure that the schools change as educational institutions?

Concern With the Whole Ability Range

The schools must divert their attention away from the top third of the ability range towards the other sections and types of pupils. The task of holding the academic and social prospects for the able has been largely attained judged by our data on delinquency and attendance rates, and by the near equivalence of the two systems on their reading scores. The task of doing the same for the bottom two-thirds of the ability range has yet to be attempted.

This is likely to involve spreading the talents of graduate teachers (like the heads of department) down through the ability range and also ensuring that in areas such as covering for absent colleagues, the same attention is given to the academic needs of lower ability children as to their higher ability counterparts. The hidden curriculum of teachers' expectations, their verbal and non-verbal cues and the other areas of the deep, emotional structure of a school will also have to reflect this same concern for all children in comprehensive schools. Negative perceptions of the lower streams and the verbal and non-verbal stigmatizing that we saw too often in the comprehensive schools must simply go. The schools must be seen to care academically and socially for these children and must be seen to care openly.

Concern For the Social As Well as the Academic

The schools must learn that whether pupils actually attend, whether they are delinquent outside the school day, whether they have positive self-conceptions and whether their pupils view themselves as in charge of their own lives are important educational goals, especially since there are a large number of lower ability pupils for whom these are the *only* educational goals that they are likely to be able to attain. This is not to say, like one head-teacher, that 'a jot of humanity is worth a hundred 'O' levels' but to argue that in a world where there is a greater chance of a child attending psychiatric hospital than of attending a university, such a reorientation of school goals towards social development seems only sensible.

This will be accomplished by a reorientation of the pastoral care system to focus much more on personal and social development and care, instead of having the control orientation that was so obvious in our comprehensive schools. Also, the pastoral care system seemed to deal more with those children actually exhibiting problematic behaviour or learning difficulties than those children who may have had social problems but who succeeded in hiding them. The quiet introverted child or the instrumentally orientated child who goes through school with a minimum of emotional involvement and development (Hargreaves, D, 1979) would be just two types of pupil that need personal and social development activities but who may not be getting them currently.

Further social development could include the headteacher taking back a pastoral role rather than delegating it, the explicit statement in school prospectuses of schools' social aims and the reduction of academic pressure on the bottom two-thirds of the ability range to permit more socially-orientated activities. An expansion of the opportunities for lower ability children to meet staff informally in clubs, societies, events and sports teams is also likely to improve adult/child relationships and therefore ultimately improve social development. Easing up on frequent promotions and demotions between streams is also an academic concession that is likely to permit the maintenance of stable pupil friendship groups over time.

In general, though, the attainment of social goals in comprehensive schools necessitates a radical reorientation of their goals by their teachers. The tendency in such schools was for all teachers, even those from the former secondary modern schools, to redefine their role as being merely an imparter of knowledge in the mould of the former grammar school teacher. Much informal interaction between teachers and pupils was therefore eliminated and many of the teachers progressively disassociated themselves from such things as playground and lunchtime supervision that had been the occasions when social interaction of various kinds usually took place. Involvement with pupils, emotional transference, expressions of feeling and a genuine concern for the pupil as a whole person must replace the former grammar school concentration on academic outcomes and consequent emotional distancing.

Reorganizing Pastoral Care

Linked to a rediscovery of concern for social development and a discovery of concern for the academic and social development of less able children should be a reconstruction of the comprehensive pastoral care system. The duality of the specialist pastoral and academic sections of a school needs to be ended by the rooting of the care system in the day-to-day activities of class teachers. The encouragement of teachers to detect any need for pastoral work in their normal day-to-day activities, and the enhancement of the power of the form teacher role (by a form keeping the same teacher throughout the school or by the development of lessons for form teacher/form interaction through, say, active tutorial work) would seem to be useful initiatives in this context. A pastoral curriculum (Marland, 1980) is also likely to be useful in integrating pastoral and academic concerns. Where pastoral problems are identified and where referral to specialist pastoral work is considered necessary, swift administrative procedures are needed to ensure a link between whatever precipitated the referral and the remedial action that is taken. Rather than the rapid resolve to suspension or referral to outside agencies, the schools need to develop a range of *internal* responses ranging through counselling, change of teacher, change of subjects, change of form, movement into a withdrawal group, movement into outside school units, suspension etc. The emphasis must be on a de-escalating pastoral system aimed at mainstreaming children as much as possible, rather than as at present on an escalating, increasingly exclusive care system that does not evoke enough within-school remedial attempts and instead 'dumps' children in the hands of outside professional agencies.

If outside help is required, though, it should be monitored and assessed and coordinated with the inside-school strategies by means of the care committees (which involve school guidance personnel, form teacher, subject teachers, etc.) that were only in embryo form in our schools. Coordinating the schools' pastoral network needs to have both senior school management attention and the efficient record keeping that is only possible with adequate secretarial assistance.

Improving School Management

It is clear that large complex organizations like comprehensive schools cannot be run by the forms of charismatic authority that headteachers have customarily used. Such authority, where motivation is by using aspects of the person, has customarily been replaced by forms of bureaucratic authority, where motivation is by using aspects of the person's role. The development of adequate bureaucratic strategies for management, usually involving giving power holders other than the headteacher a 'senior management label' and devolving much routine exercise of power to them, is clearly the start of effective comprehensive school practice.

We suspect, though, that the development of comprehensive education requires a movement towards a far more participatory style of management, as we have argued elsewhere (Reynolds, 1986a; Murgatroyd and Reynolds, 1984). The comprehensive schools' large size has led both to goal confusion and to an inconsistency of expectations as to standards of pupil attainment and behaviour amongst different teachers, as the schools became personally and ideologically fractured and fragmented institutions in the 1970s. Consequently, only the increased involvement of school staffs in the management of schools is likely to lead to consistency in these areas as the differences between persons and groups become eroded by better interpersonal communication. The holding of regular staff meetings with definite advisory/ executive power, the publication of senior management team agendas for their meetings, the encouragement of 'rank and file' teachers to join senior management teams and the setting up of teacher working parties to consider specific topics are all ways of ensuring teacher involvement in the life of the school. Good communication by means of publishing senior management team decisions, ensuring that all staff know each others' involvements through noticeboard 'weekly diaries' and the publication of staff handbooks containing basic information on staff roles, rights and responsibilities are all ways that may be effective in generating a staff group that is ideologically and personally cohesive.

Improving Links with Parents

The establishment of formal parent/teacher associations, which neither of our comprehensives had managed, is merely the first step towards enlisting parental support in the education of their children. Creating an atmosphere where informal parental visits are encouraged is also important, as is ensuring that parents can feel free to come to the school to talk about theoretically non-educational matters such as financial problems, marital problems, housing problems etc. which may have important educational implications for some of the pupils. At both formal and informal levels, parents (especially of lower ability children) will be very sensitive to how they are treated. Making comprehensive schools genuinely responsive to their parents and to their communities involves more than calling themselves 'community schools'. It involves a transformation of attitudes.

Rules, Rewards and Punishments

The eroding of some of the rules concerning 'dress, manners and morals' inherited from the grammar schools (who had in turn inherited them from the public schools) is essential to ensure low ability pupils' commitment to their schools. Truces on uniform once enforcement gets difficult from the middle of the third year at school and the permitting of 'token uniforms' such as a school tie for boys or cardigan for girls are essential, as is a reduction in rates of physical punishment which most evidence suggests simply increases levels of misbehaviour (Reynolds, 1976; British Psychological Society, 1980).

The incorporation of more fourth and fifth year pupils by spreading leadership roles down the school from the sixth-form and by similarly breaking clubs, societies and sports teams away from higher stream domination would also seem to be important, as is a reward based policy within the school which maximizes both instrumental rewards and status rewards and consequently minimizes punishments. Rewarding effort through teacher behaviour, reports, etc. must also be given an equal priority with the rewarding of attainments, and rewarding social attainment like simply succeeding at the 'nice person' role should also be given equal priority to rewarding academic attainment.

Persevering With Unstreaming and Curriculum Change

The two areas where our comprehensives had attempted changes by comparison with the selective system were the ability grouping system and the knowledge base of the school that was presented to children. That the schools had only changed in these two areas is not in itself surprising, since it was these two areas that professional discussion of comprehensive schooling had concentrated on when the system was emerging in the 1970s.

Both schools had modified the selective system's streaming and curricular patterns explicitly to help the motivation, and therefore ultimately the attainments, of lower ability children. What held both schools back from more radical experiments in the area of mixed ability teaching and in a more relevant curriculum through increased use of Mode Three CSE was the fear of adversely affecting the attainments of the able child and of generating examination passes that would not 'count' in the eyes of the public in the schools' catchment areas.

Over the decade of the 1970s, the schools themselves concluded that changes in these two areas had brought positive benefits and that, as our results confirm, the able child was still having his or her talent developed even after modification of the ability system. It seems important, then, that the schools continue to develop in this way by a further expansion of mixed ability teaching, which would also help to remove the still prevalent streaming by ability of the teachers. Massive modification of the curriculum to permit the inclusion of large quantities of more 'relevant' knowledge may well have a number of drawbacks, as we have argued ourselves (Reynolds and Sullivan, 1980), but at the least the attempt can be made to teach the 'irrelevant' school curriculum using as many 'relevant' cultural issues as possible from the social environment in which pupils live. Hargreaves' (1982) proposals for a more community-orientated curriculum may be useful in this context.

Managing Change Efficiently

Everything in the above series of policy recommendations for the comprehensive schools assumes that the schools are going to have to change if they are to successfully meet the challenge of achieving social goals and of fully developing the potential of their lower ability pupils. Even if the schools do not change in the ways that our research suggests they ought to, change will be forced on them in the next few years because of a variety of social, economic and demographic factors. The effects of falling rolls is leading to school closures, amalgamation and the grouping of schools to teach small sixth form options. The development of tertiary education will lead to the closure of school sixth-forms. The scope of central government and Manpower Services Commission interventionism is likely to continue its increase in the views of most contemporary commentators (Hunter, 1984; Simon, 1986).

All this means that schools will be having to undergo the upheavals associated with major organizational change, just as the comprehensives had to when they began to emerge in the late 1960s and early 1970s. In order that these new changes do not generate the same problems of goal direction and fragmented organizational response that marked their emergence, comprehensive schools must ensure that information on proposed changes is disseminated, that teachers are involved in decision taking about change, that the needs of different sub-groups within each school organization are taken into account when new organizations emerge and that there is perceived equity of treatment for those groups forced to respond to change. In this way, it may be possible for the reshaped comprehensive education of the 1990s to avoid the traumatic 'settling down' phase that marred the first and second years of our schools' existence.

It will be clear from the above discussion that all these recommendations are interrelated and closely linked with each other. Concern for social outcomes is bound to necessitate a concern for the low ability children who generate the majority of school social problems, which in turn is linked with the reconstruction of pastoral care. Improving school management necessitates a better management of change. Incorporating parental support and incorporating pupils to feel that they partially 'own' their schools are also linked. Whilst each of these areas of school life requires its own individual attention, only by means of a 'whole school' approach which involves change in every area of institutional functioning can the comprehensives begin the process of purposive, rather than reactive, change that has eluded them so far.

It will also be clear from the above discussion that in many respects what we are recommending for the comprehensive schools is a readoption of aspects of the secondary modern school tradition. Most accounts of these schools are of the 'school as hell' or 'school as war' variety (Hargreaves, 1967; Partridge, 1966; Woods, 1979), yet our evidence shows them as having developed highly successful strategies for the management of their children. Some of our recommendations reflect the need to cope with the size of comprehensive schools and are aimed at improving consistency, cohesion and control. More of our recommendations also — it must be said — reflect the need of the schools to discard some of their grammar school inheritance in favour of the more relaxed, less academically pressured and more relationship-orientated secondary modern approach. Secondary modern schools and their traditions were unwisely resisted against as the new schools were formed and it is time their strengths were rediscovered and blended with some of the existing grammar school traditions to generate authentic comprehensive education for all children. One school that has done this forms the basis of our next book (Reynolds and Sullivan, forthcoming).

The modern day comprehensive school is as an organization of course thoroughly understandable. Keeping grammar school rules to gain status in the community is understandable. Trying to show middle-class parents that the schools are not an academic threat to their children is understandable. Moving from informal, charismatic based forms of leadership to more bureaucratic forms is equally understandable. Equally understandable to us are some of the damaging consequences of internal school processes that we believe must be changed.

The Political Debate and Comprehensives

At the time of writing, there are a wide variety of views expressed about the future of the comprehensive school within the political system. There have been attempts to bring back selection by some Conservative-controlled local education authorities. There have been persistent attempts to discredit comprehensive schools and arguments to bring back a selective system from many right wing commentators (for example, Flew, 1983) and from pressure groups such as the National Council for Academic Standards (Cox and Marks, 1983 and 1985). Right-wing academics have made considerable play with the fact that France and Germany, who are argued to generate a more educated and skilled workforce, still retain selective education systems (Prais and Wagner, 1985). Some right wingers have also compared Northern Ireland and the rest of Britain, arguing that the higher levels of attainment reported by the Assessment of Performance Unit (APU) for the former is because of their retention of selective education.

A flavour of some current right wing views of the schools is given in the following three extracts from the speeches of contemporary Conservative politicians. *The Daily Mail* of 10 December 1985 quoted 'Schools Minister Bob Dunn' as follows:

> Comprehensive schools are failing, an Education minister said at the weekend.
>
> As a result of all-in schools, pupils now are doing worse than 20 years ago, said Schools Minister Bob Dunn.
>
> He told a Conservative Women's Organization meeting in Dartford, Kent, that the promised rise in the academic standards of children of all abilities had not been achieved.

Despite more education spending in real terms than ever before and the best yet pupil teacher ratio in schools, Mr. Dunn said most parents think the quality of schooling today is poorer in many respects than ever before.

And he said 'It seems a supreme irony that the proportion of working-class children entering our universities has actually declined since the imposition of the comprehensive.'

Nor, he claimed, did the fact that exam results are getting better mean that comprehensive schools are doing better.

'Unfortunately that does not seem to be the case', he said. 'The proportion of school-leavers achieving five or more 'O' levels and one or more 'A' levels in England rose during the fifties and sixties but then levelled off and only in the last few years has risen slowly again.

'But if the figures are closely examined, I find that it is the results of the independent schools that brought about this rising pattern.'

All the figures show, said Mr. Dunn, that a child is more likely to do better academically, whatever his ability, in a selective system with a variety of schools.

'It shows that schools which concentrate their efforts upon specific groups of children of similar ability, whatever that ability might be, are more likely to achieve more with those children than the schools that attempt to cater for everybody', he said.

Tory MP J F Pawsey spoke in the education debate in the House of Commons on 23 January 1986 as follows:

There is an interesting benchmark available to us to judge performance. In the past, results in Northern Ireland were less good than in other home counties, but that situation has been reversed, and in Ireland, despite the bombings and the terrorists, examination results are steadily improving and have become some of the best within the United Kingdom. Therefore, I think that the House should ask itself what is going right in the Province. Why do they alone swim against the tide? Can it be — shock horror — that it is due to the retention of selective education? Can that be the difference? Judged by the quality of examination results, it certainly could well be.

I wonder whether the House has the courage to accept that perhaps selective schools — and remember they exist in France, Germany and the Soviet Union — hold the key to excellence in education. Perhaps my right hon. Friend should consider positive discrimination to enable the emergence of centres of excellence throughout the United Kingdom. Mainland standards might then stand more favourable comparison with those in Northern Ireland.

Conservative MP Alan Howarth expressed similar sentiments in the same debate:

> Over the past twenty years we have seen centuries of slowly nurtured educational tradition uprooted. We have seen the abolition of the grammar schools. Since the recent county council elections when I am afraid some of the citizens of south Warwickshire were soft-headed enough to vote Liberal and let Labour into control in shire hall, even the grammar school that Shakespeare attended is under threat because they propose to abolish it.

There is little that has been done, or proposed, by the Conservative government which in our view makes the generation of improved forms of comprehensive schooling more likely. The assisted places scheme, giving places for more able pupils at independent schools, is creaming able pupils off from the schools and the loss of only a small number of such pupils (such as the current 1 per cent nationally), may have dramatic effects upon the practicality of certain options and on the intellectual balance of a school. Proposals to reintroduce direct grant schools, to centrally fund 'Crown schools' in the inner cities and to set up a network of science and technology-based schools, also in the inner cities, will have the same effects.

Other policies that have been introduced have merely intensified the already existing pressure towards an over-concern with academic standards and pupils' academic attainments at the schools. Giving parents a greater power on governing bodies, as in the 1986 Education Act, and giving parents the right to express a preference for the school their child attends, as in the 1980 Education Act, is likely to lead to a further concentration on the academic by the schools, given the evidence we have on what parents want of their schools. Publishing academic, but not social, results is likely to have the same effect and voucher schemes, where parents can choose their child's state or independent sector school, would both intensify this academic pressure on schools and also probably encourage the comprehensives to keep many of the alienating school rules which appeal to parents but not to pupils.

The Conservative concern for the able child and for academic results is likely to magnify the schools' failure with their less able pupils and with their social outcomes. Present governmental policies are diametrically opposite to what is needed to generate improved comprehensive education, since the education of the able is not the schools' problem.

Labour party policy on comprehensive schools is in our view also not adequate to deal with the schools' problems. In recent party pronouncements (Radice, 1986; Kinnock, 1986), there is an emphasis upon getting small class sizes, upon adequate resourcing of books and equipment and upon better maintenance of plant. The left continues to believe that the system's problems are primarily material, yet our evidence suggests the problems are rooted in the organization and culture of schooling and in its quality rather than its quantity. How to change the schools, how to modify their internal organization and how to get what is almost a cultural revolution in the teaching profession's behaviour, expectations and attitudes has not been addressed.

The current concern with standards and educational attainment, and the portrayal of the system as able to generate a return for the wider society at the same time as social justice for the disadvantaged groups has an ominously 1960s ring about it. Now — just as then — no formal internal school organization is specified for the comprehensive school. Now — just as then — no acknowledgement is made of the informal culture of schooling and of the ethos that may be so determinate of the success or failure of the educational policies legislated for by central government. Now — just as then — the evaluation, change and improvement of schools is somehow to come through a mix of increased centralization, greater parental power and a parental Ombudsman to answer complaints, yet there is no evidence that this leverage upon the system will be able to reach and change internal school organization and practices any more than it has managed in the past.

Now, just as the 1960s, there is no specification of what a comprehensive school actually looks like in terms of content and process for teachers and pupils. In the absence of clear political and legislative definitions of what comprehensive schools are in terms of organization, goals and means, the perpetuation of the existing pseudo-comprehensives seems inevitable. It appears from all this that Labour really isn't learning.

Concern with levels of spending and with the nature of parental/local government/central government power or leverage in the system that characterize the existing debate are the hallmarks of an essentially sterile set of political attitudes to the schools, since what comes out of the system is clearly determined neither by the resources available to it nor by the formal power relations under which it is operated, since there is substantial autonomy at the level of the individual school (Reynolds, 1984a). How to affect directly what goes on in the particular 'black box' of people and policies that we call a school is what we turn to now.

Educational Policy and the Comprehensive School

Since none of the available range of policies outlined by the political parties seems to us to come close to what is required, we are perhaps duty bound to offer here our own comments on what may be necessary to improve the schools.

Evaluation

At the level of the individual school, there should be publication of school delinquency rates, attendance levels, vandalism levels and referral rate to outside educational provision. These should be published for each ability range, since the school experience enjoyed by pupils may be different in the different ability ranges (Reynolds, 1986b). At the LEA level, there should be attempts to evaluate school performance on this wider range of outcomes by means of input/output analysis, where testing of children as they enter and as they leave school enables the identification of those schools that are underperforming by comparison with what would have been expected from the quality of their intakes. Whilst there are clearly a large number of LEAs already doing routine monitoring of this kind (Gipps *et al*, 1983), there has been some concern over the choice of evaluative tests, the practice of only testing parts of the ability range and the absence of measurement of social outcomes. The systematic attempts by the Inner London Education Authority to control for variations in the quality of school catchment areas in their 'league tables' would seem to be something of a model for other LEAs to follow.

Change Strategies

Precisely what is done to help the underperforming schools improve is clearly a matter of some importance. There is evidence from both the United States (Schmuck, 1978), and Britain (Bolam and Porter, 1976), that there is a large credibility gap between schools and all outsiders that attempt to influence what goes on in the school. The problems of attempting change in problem-prone schools are likely to be even greater, since all sorts of defences against change are likely to exist (Reynolds, 1986a; Murgatroyd and Gray, 1982). Teachers may externalize the blame for their problems on to outside factors like the catchment area, the parents and the pupils.

There are the fantasies — that change is someone else's job. There are the 'clingons' of past practice — we've always done it this way. There is the 'safety in numbers' block — individuals wanting or needing to change are held back by the large number of other teachers that they are linked with who are resistant to change. There is fear of failure — all change in schools involves risk, yet many teachers are reluctant to risk the potential improvement that change could bring to their schools because of the fear that the changes may fail. The schools also employ scapegoats successfully — their own problems are seen as due to 'the state of society'. The schools are also knowledge deficient — about alternative ways of organizing, about the outputs of their existing practices and about the processes required to get any changes in the school organizations. The schools also are used to closed leadership, where power resides in a small number of hands — solutions are expected from those in authority rather than being seen as potentially lying in the hands of others within the organization.

It is clear that conventional in-service training is not the answer. Threatened or insecure staff groups are, in our experience, the least likely to take up any form of in-service exercise. Such an exercise, if it conventionally involves taking teachers away from their schools, is likely to be centred upon trainers' desires rather than teachers' needs. School-focussed INSET on the other hand may be productive of change (Phillips and Davie, 1985).

The LEA advisory services are highly unlikely to be able to change the ineffective school. They have conventionally been involved in curriculum development, not in the organizational or management areas which they have regarded as the province of the individual school headteacher. Many of them have no experience of comprehensive schools, or of management other than as a head of department on the academic side of a school. They have traditionally adopted a highly voluntaristic approach to their schools which may not be an appropriate way of ensuring that the problem school actually improves (Pearce, 1986).

The Inspectorate, too, are unlikely to be able to change poorly performing schools. They are often shrewd in their judgments of internal school processes, management competence and school ethos or atmosphere, yet recent evidence (Gray and Hannon, 1986) suggests that they make no systematic attempt to allow for variations in the raw material that schools are getting. Comparisons of individual schools are often against national or LEA or other schools' standards, which is meaningless unless one allows for variations in the pupils that the individual school is getting.

It is clear that attempts offered to these schools must be sensitive to the internal dynamics and relationships that exist within the under-attaining school. Any attempt to help must therefore be premised on the basis that the school and its staff actually 'own' the change attempt, so that the school will feel secure. Outsiders can become 'consultants' to the school, taking its problems as it sees them, resourcing the school with knowledge about what to do and helping the school evaluate what the effects of any changes have been. Networking — putting the school in touch with people who can help with action and ideas at a local level — replaces the old, ineffective 'top-down' change strategies. Consulting and networking in this way is empowerment, giving to schools the capacity to go for personal and institutional change and get the personal growth that can result from successful institutional change (Murgatroyd and Reynolds, 1985).

In additon to maximizing the chances that change attempts will be successful by letting the schools own them, the change attempts themselves must concentrate upon different areas of school life. Resources, the formal organization and the curriculum vessel that contains the knowledge are all areas where the comprehensive schools attempted to change their internal school processes, yet our research suggests that it is the culture of the schools, their personal relationships and the 'deep structure' of their relationships and feelings that must be a focus for reform. Again, if one hopes to look at and ultimately change such delicate areas, those whom one hopes to change need very delicate handling in the change attempts.

Creative Conflict

We need to evaluate, then, and to empower the comprehensive schools facing problems. For certain schools this will not be enough to produce change, since the process of blame of children, of catchment area and of parents may be too entrenched to break. The defences that all vulnerable organizations build up may be too strong.

In this case, members of professional groups that relate to schools will have to indulge in a little 'creative conflict' with them. Social workers can be change agents by reporting on schools at court hearings for non-attendance for example — schools can be taken to court in this way. EWOs can take parents and children's views back to their schools. Withdrawal or off-site units can pressure their high referral rate schools. Educational psychologists can collect data, act as an advocate for the child against the school, tell headteachers about their less than competent colleagues, work with individual teachers, be based in schools and alert other professionals to the 'problem schools'.

At the moment, members of professions actually do little of this, although there is some discussion about it (Gillham, 1979 and 1981; Reynolds, 1984b). Professionals are part of an apparatus which exists to ensure the maintenance of the problem school rather than its change. They exist to help the problem school by dealing with its problems as due to personal or family problems rather than as a normal reaction by pupils to abnormal schooling, as in the case of special units (Ford *et al*, 1983), or many other outside-school solutions (Topping, 1983).

A Comprehensive Vision

In all these policy initiatives at the different levels of the educational system, a vision of the authentic comprehensive school should be kept in mind. This school must aim for the academic and social development of all its pupils. It must be effectively managed as a collectivity to ensure adequate social control. It must be consistent, cohesive and giving of identity in an uncertain world, with a corpus of knowledge that all children have in common. It must therefore be universalistic, giving to a degree the same experience to all children.

It must also, however, be selective in its organization giving different children and different ability ranges a selectively different experience. The left has customarily urged a 'steampress' model of comprehensives where '... all children are entitled to the same broad types of experience' because '... unless we try to develop in them all the same broad types of understanding, we are perpetuating a recipe for individual dissatisfaction and social unrest' (Smith, 1979, p. 189). Similar views can be found in Chitty (1979), Marsden (1971) and a host of other egalitarians.

Yet to impose uniformity of *provision* when it is quite clear from our findings that actual pupil *needs* may be different in different ability ranges is to substitute dogma for sense. Our middle ability children, for example, may well need specific policy targeting, since whilst in the secondary modern schools they were at the top of the ability range but when in comprehensive school may suffer from feelings of inferiority when brought up in close proximity to former grammar school children. The low ability child also may need a slightly different curriculum, or a greater investment of pastoral care time or perhaps different classroom teaching methods to develop his or her potential.

We do not agree with crude left-wing visions of the comprehensive school as a universal, common experience for all. Socialism is, after all, about individuals being able to give of their different abilities to a collectivity that gives to them according to their different needs. We also do not agree with the extreme forms of selectivity under one roof which characterize Conservative visions of the schools, with a radically different curriculum and ethos existing for the top and lower parts of the ability range.

For us, neither crude left nor right-wing visions of the school are sensible. Left-wing visions would generate too much uniformity — right-wing visions too many social differences. For us, the comprehensive school is to be both universalistic *and* selectivistic, with a common universal experience that is partially selectivily modified or 'topped up' according to the different needs of portions of the ability ranges and of individuals within them. Our desired comprehensives are neither one model or the other — they incorporate elements of both. Since both the health service and social security system have been until recently run on the basis of a universal base, selectively modified to suit the needs of different age, gender and class groups, there should be no problem in establishing a philosophical and political consensus for these arrangements in the education system.

The Comprehensive School and Academic Debate

It would be wrong of us to finish our conclusions and recommendations without briefly looking at the implications of our work for the academic study of the sociology of education and of school effectiveness.

For the former, the evidence suggests that the educational system has a considerable degree of autonomy in how it responds to outside political and economic pressures. The history of comprehensive schools is one of specification of goals by the 'macro' systems of political and economic life and of virtually no specification of organizational means from outside the educational system, which left the system free to cope as best it could. In a similar way as to how the secondary modern schools of our early work used their freedom to develop different institutional responses to fulfil their 'child minding' role (Reynolds and Sullivan, 1979), the comprehensives in our work used their freedom to develop their own ineffective organizational strategies to deliver higher attainment levels. Crucially, these micro level organizational strategies pursued by the comprehensive schools nationally and locally have had an impact upon the 'macrosocial' local and national social systems, as the schools' outputs of a more anti-social, delinquent pupil peer group have evoked differing control strategies from the local and national state apparatuses. In a very real sense, the educational system from our work can be seen as both determined by wider economic, political and social forces and yet independent of them, acting back upon the macrosocial forces that have moulded and influenced it. It has a relative autonomy (Reynolds, 1984a, King, 1985).

This perspective of the partial autonomy of the educational system from outside constraints is of course fundamentally different from the perspectives that have predominated during the last fifteen years of the discipline (see review in Reynolds and Sullivan, 1980). 'Macro' level analyses have stressed the dependence of the system on outside forces that constrain it to be reproductive of the present society, as in the determinist analysis of Althusser (1971) and the 'correspondence' thesis of Bowles and Gintis (1976). 'Micro' level work into classrooms and into teacher and pupil interaction has stressed the freedom that exists to create new meanings and to generate transformed educational practices in every classroom (Young, 1971).

Work at the 'meso' or school level, where macro forces meet the micro and where teachers and pupils have micro level freedoms, is in urgent need of expansion. From the school one can look out to the constraints of local and central government policy and at the economic, political and social factors that determine it. From the school, one can look down to the classroom where outside school factors are mediated to pupils through their interactions with teachers. One sees freedoms and one sees determinations; humans are influenced by outside school forces and one sees humans as influencing by their coping strategies these constraints on their lives in interactive feedback. Work at this 'meso' level may well be able to generate a more empirically informed, more policy relevant and more intellectually coherent British sociology of education than has been exhibited for the past fifteen years.

For the school effectiveness movement, our findings are in many ways highly reassuring. Firstly, our findings of considerable *system* effects upon pupils are supportive of those who have argued that individual *schools* have effects upon pupils (Reynolds, 1985a; Rutter, 1983). Secondly, our findings on the somewhat different experiences of different ability ranges are supportive of those who have found similar findings with school against school comparisons (Gray, Jesson and Jones, 1986; Aitken and Longford, 1986). Thirdly, our findings on which factors are associated with inferior comprehensive system performance are very similar to those seen in individual studies of ineffective schools in Britain and America (see reviews in Rutter, 1983; Anderson, 1982; Reynolds, 1985a).

Comprehensives were of larger size, with less cohesion on goals and means, had higher pupil/staff mobility, less collegiality in staff relations, had stricter ruler enforcement, a split pastoral/academic system, had lower levels of parental and pupil involvement and higher levels of social punishment. The only factors the schools possessed which might have led to greater effectiveness were the modification of the ability grouping system and its higher academic press. Ironically, the schools' lower class sizes, higher per pupil expenditure and vastly more adequate buildings did not lead to improved outcomes, as has been shown in the majority of studies in this area thus far.

At a time when school effectiveness research is in need of new impetus and self-confidence after a period of considerable doubt (Reynolds and Reid, 1985), our findings can be seen as in many ways reassuring in the support they give to current notions of the effective school.

The Comprehensive School and Contemporary Society

Our final conclusions must relate to the continuing debate about the direction of modern society. Over the last decade the community which we study has undergone the same profound changes as others in that the importance of community has declined. Slum clearance that breaks up extended families, the effects of unemployment in fragmenting men and women's occupational cultures and the death of collective institutions like churches and clubs have led to a more fragmented society and the concern with instrumentality has increased this trend. The upper groups in schools and the upper groups in society have had attention and rewards showered upon them, not the lower. Getting on past your colleagues has replaced getting on with them (see Reynolds and Sullivan, 1982, for further speculations on this theme).

Comprehensive schools have reflected these trends and then gone on to mould them further. They are concerned for their upper groups, for instrumental, rather than social, rewards and they have generated fragmented, not integrated, children by their own fragmentation and absence of community. The schools have been reproductive in their effects.

To argue that the schools should become more concerned with all their children and to argue that social goals are as important as academic goals in modern society may currently be unfashionable in many quarters. But unless the schools manage to give to all children social development that parts of the system of education have managed to in the past together with the intellectual development that other parts of the education system have delivered, the future of British society will in our view be bleak. To use their autonomy as institutions to transform the wider society, rather than simply magnify the already existing unhealthy social trends, must be the new comprehensive experiment of the late 1980s.

Appendices

Appendix 1

Intake and Raw Outcome Data for Two Systems

VARIABLE	NUMBER OF CASES	MEAN	STANDARD DEVIATION	STANDARD ERROR	* * *	T VALUE	2-TAIL PROB.
EXTRAVERSION					*		
GROUP 1	101	16.9703	5.047	0.502	*		
					*	−0.63	0.527
GROUP 2	227	17.3833	5.631	0.374	*		
					*		
NEUROTICISM					*		
GROUP 1	101	13.4851	5.691	0.566	*		
					*	0.47	0.639
GROUP 2	227	13.1982	4.834	0.321	*		
					*		
LIE SCALE					*		
GROUP 1	101	3.0792	2.473	0.246	*		
					*	−0.50	0.619
GROUP 2	227	3.4053	6.366	0.423	*		
					*		
READ A					*		
GROUP 1	101	36.8020	12.508	1.245	*		
					*	0.58	0.566
GROUP 2	227	35.9383	12.572	0.834	*		
					*		
READ B					*		
GROUP 1	101	16.5545	6.881	0.685	*		
					*	0.05	0.963
GROUP 2	227	16.5154	7.142	0.474	*		
					*		
MATHS					*		
GROUP 1	101	23.8515	10.725	1.067	*		
					*	1.50	0.135
GROUP 2	227	21.9824	10.290	0.683	*		
					*		

MATRICES					*		
GROUP 1	101	37.7921	11.125	1.107	*	2.14	0.033
GROUP 2	227	34.6388	12.823	0.851	*		
RAW ERT					*		
GROUP 1	101	100.5545	28.893	2.875	*	3.39	0.001
GROUP 2	227	87.4317	33.734	2.239	*		
AGE ADJUSTED ERT					*		
GROUP 1	101	100.2673	14.508	1.444	*	2.95	0.003
GROUP 2	227	94.5022	17.080	1.134	*		
SUB ERT 1 (RAW)					*		
GROUP 1	101	24.7228	5.958	0.593	*	3.61	0.000
GROUP 2	227	21.7048	7.406	0.492	*		
SUB ERT 2 (RAW)					*		
GROUP 1	101	23.2673	8.621	0.858	*	3.11	0.002
GROUP 2	227	19.8634	9.384	0.623	*		
SUB ERT 3 (RAW)					*		
GROUP 1	101	21.1683	5.024	0.500	*	3.62	0.000
GROUP 2	227	18.4053	6.902	0.458	*		
SUB ERT 4 (RAW)					*		
GROUP 1	101	17.3762	8.047	0.801	*	1.43	0.155
GROUP 2	227	15.9427	8.563	0.568	*		
SUB ERT 5 (RAW)					*		
GROUP 1	101	13.6535	5.347	0.532	*	2.30	0.022
GROUP 2	227	12.1101	5.735	0.381	*		
INT EXT CONTROL					*		
GROUP 1	101	24.1386	3.803	0.378	*	12.50	0.000
GROUP 2	227	17.8634	4.361	0.289	*		
LOCUS UP					*		
GROUP 1	101	12.8218	2.447	0.243	*	9.55	0.000
GROUP 2	227	9.8678	2.646	0.176	*		

LOCUS DOWN					*		
GROUP 1	101	11.3168	2.315	0.230	*		
					*	10.14	0.000
GROUP 2	227	7.8282	2.808	0.186	*		
					*		
FINLAY SCALE 1 (ASI)					*		
GROUP 1	101	70.7822	14.615	1.454	*		
					*	4.32	0.000
GROUP 2	227	63.3833	14.202	0.943	*		
					*		
F SUB 1					*		
GROUP 1	101	38.8020	7.725	0.769	*		
					*	3.28	0.001
GROUP 2	227	35.6784	8.073	0.536	*		
					*		
F SUB 2					*		
GROUP 1	101	31.8515	8.066	0.803	*		
					*	4.64	0.000
GROUP 2	227	27.6608	7.323	0.486	*		
					*		
FINLAY SCALE 2 (NSI)					*		
GROUP 1	101	55.9802	12.520	1.246	*		
					*	1.07	0.287
GROUP 2	227	54.2819	13.642	0.905	*		
					*		
NSI SUB 1					*		
GROUP 1	101	14.6337	3.778	0.376	*		
					*	0.78	0.434
GROUP 2	227	14.2775	3.806	0.253	*		
					*		
NSI SUB 2					*		
GROUP 1	101	11.7228	3.482	0.346	*		
					*	1.81	0.071
GROUP 2	227	10.9648	3.511	0.233	*		
					*		
NSI SUB 3					*		
GROUP 1	101	14.9505	3.664	0.365	*		
					*	1.61	0.109
GROUP 2	227	14.2423	3.693	0.245	*		
					*		
NSI SUB 4					*		
GROUP 1	101	14.6139	4.226	0.421	*		
					*	−0.44	0.637
GROUP 2	227	14.8326	4.061	0.270	*		
					*		

Appendix 2

Pearson Product Moment Correlations Between Intake and Outcome Variables

	RAW ERT	AGE ERT	SUB ERT 1	SUB ERT 2	SUB ERT 3	SUB ERT 4	SUB ERT 5	INT EXT	LOCUS UP	LOCUS DN
EXTRAV	0.0879 (328) P = 0.056	0.4040 (328) P = 0.000	0.2353 (328) P = 0.000	0.0881 (328) P = 0.056	0.2477 (328) P = 0.000	0.3276 (328) P = 0.000	0.2505 (328) P = 0.000	0.1957 (328) P = 0.000	-0.0786 (328) P = 0.078	-0.706 (328) P = 0.101
NEUROT	-0.0654 (328) P = 0.119	-0.1065 (328) P = 0.027	-0.0218 (328) P = 0.347	-0.0546 (328) P = 0.162	-0.0447 (328) P = 0.210	-0.1193 (328) P = 0.015	-0.1200 (328) P = 0.015	-0.0208 (328) P = 0.354	0.0291 (328) P = 0.300	-0.0227 (328) P = 0.341
READA	0.6628 (328) P = 0.000	0.6023 (328) P = 0.000	0.6224 (328) P = 0.000	0.6313 (328) P = 0.000	0.6224 (328) P = 0.000	0.5387 (328) P = 0.000	0.5590 (328) P = 0.000	0.2508 (328) P = 0.000	0.2619 (328) P = 0.000	0.1518 (328) P = 0.003
READB	0.6195 (328) P = 0.000	0.7487 (328) P = 0.000	0.6052 (328) P = 0.000	0.6078 (328) P = 0.000	0.6382 (328) P = 0.000	0.6549 (328) P = 0.000	0.6290 (328) P = 0.000	0.3281 (328) P = 0.000	0.1849 (328) P = 0.000	0.1177 (328) P = 0.017
MATHS	0.5802 (328) P = 0.000	0.6775 (328) P = 0.000	0.5819 (328) P = 0.000	0.5349 (328) P = 0.000	0.5949 (328) P = 0.000	0.6053 (328) P = 0.000	0.6102 (328) P = 0.000	0.3871 (328) P = 0.000	0.2644 (328) P = 0.000	0.1684 (328) P = 0.001
MATRICES	0.4860 (328) P = 0.000	0.4679 (328) P = 0.000	0.4536 (328) P = 0.000	0.4645 (328) P = 0.000	0.4420 (328) P = 0.000	0.3872 (328) P = 0.000	0.4287 (328) P = 0.000	0.2834 (328) P = 0.000	0.2333 (328) P = 0.000	0.2307 (328) P = 0.000

	FINLAY 1	FSUB 1	FSUB 2	FINLAY 2	NSISUB 1	NSISUB 2	NSISUB 3	NSISUB 4
EXTRAV	-0.0261 (328) P = 0.319	-0.0533 (328) P = 0.168	0.0094 (328) P = 0.433	-0.0073 (328) P = 0.448	-0.0033 (328) P = 0.476	0.0152 (328) P = 0.392	-0.0347 (328) P = 0.265	-0.0030 (328) P = 0.478
NEUROT	-0.523 (328) P = 0.172	-0.0713 (328) P = 0.099	-0.0305 (328) P = 0.291	-0.0623 (328) P = 0.130	-0.0370 (328) P = 0.252	-0.0737 (328) P = 0.091	-0.0262 (328) P = 0.318	-0.0662 (328) P = 0.116
READA	0.4828 (328) P = 0.000	0.4337 (328) P = 0.000	0.4511 (328) P = 0.000	0.4619 (328) P = 0.000	-0.4093 (328) P = 0.000	0.4015 (328) P = 0.000	0.3855 (328) P = 0.000	0.4366 (328) P = 0.000
READB	0.4127 (328) P = 0.000	0.3490 (328) P = 0.000	0.4099 (328) P = 0.000	0.4032 (328) P = 0.000	0.3478 (328) P = 0.000	0.3713 (328) P = 0.000	0.3285 (328) P = 0.000	0.3768 (328) P = 0.000
MAFS	0.4059 (328) P = 0.000	0.3386 (328) P = 0.000	0.4083 (328) P = 0.000	0.3905 (328) P = 0.000	-0.3418 (328) P = 0.000	0.3703 (328) P = 0.000	0.3401 (328) P = 0.000	0.3270 (328) P = 0.000
MATRICES	0.4224 (328) P = 0.000	0.3596 (328) P = 0.000	0.4274 (328) P = 0.000	0.3906 (328) P = 0.000	0.3371 (328) P = 0.000	0.3497 (328) P = 0.000	0.3592 (328) P = 0.000	0.3344 (328) P = 0.000

Appendix 3

Multiple Regressions of Intake and Major Outcome Variables

This was a longitudinal study in which intake data could be used to predict outcomes. We therefore chose to use stepwise multiple regression of outcome variables on the intake variables to obtain the necessary weights for each variable to produce a prediction.

The procedure involved: (a) the calculation of a stepwise multiple regression for each outcome variable using all of the intake variables; (b) the allocation of weights to each intake variable to produce a prediction for each outcome variable; and (c) the examination of residuals resulting both from the regression and from the comparison of actual and predicted scores. These analyses were completed at the level of the whole sample. The four regressions now follow.

DEPENDENT VARIABLE   AGE ERT

VARIABLE	MULTIPLE R	SUMMARY TABLE R SQUARE	RSQ CHANGE	SIMPLE R	B
READB	0.74870	0.56055	0.56055	0.74870	1.344242
MATRICES	0.77354	0.59836	0.03781	0.46788	0.2280883
MAFS	0.78374	0.61425	0.01589	0.67749	0.3527860
NEUROT	0.78978	0.62376	0.00950	-0.10652	-0.299698
READA	0.79092	0.62556	0.00180	0.60227	-0.9819629D-01
(CONSTANT)					65.51035

DEPENDENT VARIABLE   INT-EXT CONTROL

VARIABLE	MULTIPLE R	SUMMARY TABLE R SQUARE	RSQ CHANGE	SIMPLE R	B
MAFS	0.38712	0.14986	0.14986	0.38712	0.1516391
MATRICES	0.40583	0.16469	0.01483	0.28344	0.5644683D-01
READB	0.40848	0.16686	0.00216	0.32806	0.1179306
READA	0.41794	0.17467	0.00781	0.25082	-0.6182124D-01
NEUROT	0.41803	0.17475	0.00008	-0.02077	-0.8914517D-02
(CONSTANT)					14.77256

DEPENDENT VARIABLE   FINLAYSON SCALE 1

VARIABLE	MULTIPLE R	SUMMARY TABLE R SQUARE	RSQ CHANGE	SIMPLE R	B
READA	0.48275	0.23305	0.23305	0.48275	0.3273266
MATRICES	0.54822	0.30055	0.06750	0.42242	0.3097487
EXTRAV	0.58965	0.34769	0.04714	-0.02613	-0.8126500
READB	0.60141	0.36169	0.01401	0.41270	0.3820100
MAFS	0.60377	0.36454	0.00284	0.40586	0.1230737
NEUROT	0.60445	0.36537	0.00083	-0.05232	-0.8463608D-01
(CONSTANT)					48.83865

DEPENDENT VARIABLE   FINLAYSON SCALE 2

VARIABLE	MULTIPLE R	SUMMARY TABLE R SQUARE	RSQ CHANGE	SIMPLE R	B
READA	0.46186	0.21332	0.21332	0.46186	0.2763935
MATRICES	0.51775	0.26806	0.05475	0.39063	0.2481119
EXTRAV	0.55080	0.30338	0.03532	-0.00727	-0.6559603
READB	0.56399	0.31809	0.01470	0.40316	0.3530339
MAFS	0.56619	0.32057	0.00248	0.39047	0.1037631
NEUROT	0.56771	0.32229	0.00172	-0.06230	-0.1105717
(CONSTANT)					40.57606

Bibliography

ACKER, S. (1982) 'No woman's land: British sociology of education 1960–1979', *Sociological Review* 29, 1, pp. 77–104.

AITKEN, M. and LONGFORD, N. (1986) 'Statistical modelling issues in school effectiveness studies', *Journal of the Royal Statistical Society*, Series A, 144, 1.

ALTHUSSER, L. (1971) 'Ideology and ideological state apparatuses' reprinted in COSIN, B.R (Ed.) *Education, Structure and Society*, Harmondsworth, Penguin.

ANDERSON, C.A. (1982) 'The search for school climate: A review of the research', *Review of Educational Research*, 52, 3, pp. 368–420.

ASSESSMENT OF PERFORMANCE UNIT (APU) (1982a) *Mathematical Development, Primary Report 3*, London, HMSO.

ASSESSMENT OF PERFORMANCE UNIT (APU) (1982b) *Mathematical Development, Secondary Report 2*, London, HMSO.

ASSESSMENT OF PERFORMANCE UNIT (APU) (1982c) *Language Performance in Schools, Primary Report 1*, London, HMSO.

ASSESSMENT OF PERFORMANCE UNIT (APU) (1982d) *Language Performance in Schools, Secondary Report 1*, London, HMSO.

ASSESSMENT OF PERFORMANCE UNIT (APU) (1982e) *Science in Schools, Primary Report 1*, London, HMSO.

ASSESSMENT OF PERFORMANCE UNIT (APU) (1983) *Science in Schools, Secondary Report 1*, London, HMSO.

BALDWIN, R.W. (1975) *The Great Comprehensive Gamble*, Manchester, Helios Press.

BALDWIN, R.W. (1977) 'The dissolution of the grammar school', in COX, C.B. and BOYSON, R. (Eds) *Black Paper 1977*, London Critical Quarterly.

BALDWIN, R.W. (1979) Report in *Sunday Times*, 9 December.

BALL, S. (1981) *Beachside Comprehensive*, Cambridge, Cambridge University Press.

BALL, S. (1985) 'School politics, teachers' careers and education change: a case study of becoming a comprehensive school', in BARTON, L. and WALKER, S. (Eds) *Education and Social Change*, London, Croom Helm.

BANKS, O. and FINLAYSON, D.S. (1973) *Success and Failure in the Secondary School*, London, Methuen.

BARKER, B. (1986) *Rescuing the Comprehensive Experience*, Milton Keynes, Open University Press.

BELLABY, P. (1976) *The Sociology of Comprehensive Schooling*, London, Methuen.

BENN, C. and SIMON, B. (1970) *Half Way There*, Harmondsworth, Penguin.

BERNSTEIN, B. (1959) 'A public language: Some sociological determinants of linguistic form', in *British Journal of Sociology*, 10, 4.

BEYNON, J. (1985) *Initial Encounters in the Secondary School*, Lewes, Falmer Press.

BILSKI, R. (1971) 'Ideology and the comprehensive school', *Political Quarterly*, 42, 3.

BOLAM, R. and PORTER, J. (1976) *Innovation and In-Service Education and Training of Teachers in the United Kingdom*, Paris, OECD.

BOWLES, S. and GINTIS, H. (1976) *Schooling in Capitalist America*, London, Routledge and Kegan Paul.

BOYSON, R. (1974) *Oversubscribed: The Story of Highbury Grove*, London, Ward Lock Educational.

BRITISH PSYCHOLOGICAL SOCIETY (1980) *Report of a Working Party on Corporal Punishment in Schools*, Leicester, BPS.

BRONFENBRENNER, U. (1979) *The Ecology of Human Development*, Cambridge, MA, Harvard University Press.

BUDGE, D. (1986) 'Not proven, m'lud' *Times Educational Supplement*, 27 June, pp 12–13.

BURGESS, R.G. (1983) *Experiencing Comprehensive Education: A Study of Bishop Macgregor School*. London, Methuen.

BUSWELL, C. (1984) 'A comprehensive sixth form' in BALL, S.J. (Ed.) *Comprehensive Schooling: A Reader*, Lewes, Falmer Press.

BYRNE, D. and WILLIAMSON, B. (1975) *The Poverty of Education*, Oxford, Martin Robertson.

CAMPBELL, D.T. and STANLEY, J.C. (1963) *Experimental and Quasi Experimental Designs for Research*, Chicago, Rand McNally.

CENTRAL ADVISORY COUNCIL FOR EDUCATION (1959) *15–18 (Crowther Report)*, London, H.M.S.O.

CHITTY, C. (1979) 'Inside the secondary school: problems and prospects', in RUBENSTEIN, D. (Ed.) *Education and Equality*, Harmondsworth, Penguin.

CHOPPIN, B. (1985) 'Is education getting better?', reprinted in *Evaluation in Education*, 9, 1, pp. 91–102.

COCHRANE, A. L. (1972) *Effectiveness and Efficiency*, Oxford, Nuffield Principal Hospital Trust.

COOK, T.D. and CAMPBELL, D.T. (1975) 'The design and conduct of quasi-experiments and true experiments in field settings', in DUNNETTE, M.D. (Ed.) *Handbook of Industrial and Organizational Psychology*, Chicago, Rand McNally.

CORBISHLEY, P., EVANS, J. and DAVIES, B. (1981) 'Teacher strategies and pupil identities in mixed ability curricula: A note on concepts and some examples from maths', in BARTON, L. and WALKER, S. (Eds) *Schools, Teachers and Teaching*, Lewes, Falmer Press.

COX, C. and MARKS, J. (1983) *Standards in English Schools: First Report*, London, National Council for Educational Standards.

COX, C. and MARKS, J. (1985) *Standards in English Schools: Second Report*, London, National Council for Educational Standards.

COX, C. and MARKS, J. (1986) *Examination Results in ILEA Schools*, London, National Council for Educational Standards.

COX, C.B. and BOYSON, R. (1977) *Black Paper 1977*, London, Critical Quarterly.

CRANDALL, V.C., KATOVSKY, W. and CRANDALL, V.J. (1965) 'Children's belief in their control of reinforcements in intellectual-academic situations', *Child Development*, 36, pp. 90–109.

CROSLAND, C.A.R. (1974) *Socialism Now*, London, Jonathan Cape.

DANIELS, J.C. and DIACK, H. (1974) *The Standard Reading Tests*, London, Chatto and Windsor.

DAVIE, R. *et al* (1972) *From Birth to Seven*, London, Longmans.

DAVIES, I. (1967) *A Certain School*, Cowbridge, Cowbridge Press.

DAVIS, D. (1984) 'To each according to his class', *Times Educational Supplement*, 6 January, p. 4.

DAVIS, R. (1967) *The Grammar School*, Harmondsworth, Penguin.

DAWSON, P. (1981) *Making a Comprehensive Work: The Road from Bomb Alley*, Oxford, Basil Blackwell.

DENSCOMBE, M. (1984) 'Control, controversy and the comprehensive school' in BALL, S.J. (Ed.) *Comprehensive Schooling: A Reader*, Lewes, Falmer Press.

DENT, H.C. (1970) *A Century of English Education* (reissue), London, Longman.

DEPARTMENT OF EDUCATION AND SCIENCE (1983) *School Standards and Spending: Statistical Analysis*. London, DES

DEPARTMENT OF EDUCATION AND SCIENCE (1984a) *Comments on Standards in English Schools by Statistical Branch*, unpublished paper.

DEPARTMENT OF EDUCATION AND SCIENCE (1984b) *School Standards and Spending: Statistical Analysis. A Further Appreciation*. London, DES

DEPARTMENT OF EDUCATION AND SCIENCE (1986) *Education Statistics for the United Kingdom, 1985*, London, HMSO

DERRICK, T. (1980), 'Some recent trends in British educational research', *Bulletin of the British Psychological Society*, 33, September, pp. 341–3.

DINGLE, A. (1984) 'Dragging up the able', *Times Educational Supplement*, 3 February, p. 22.

DIXON, S. (1962) *Some aspects of school life and progress in a comprehensive school relative to pupil social background*, unpublished MA thesis, University of London.

DOUGLAS, J.W.B. (1964) *The Home and the School*, London, Panther.

DOUGLAS, J.W.B. (1968) *All Our Future*, London, Panther.

EGGLESTON, J. (1967) 'Some environmental correlates of extended secondary education in England', *Comparative Education*, 3.

EVANS, J. (1985) *Teaching in Transition*, Milton Keynes, Open University Press.

EYSENCK, S.B.G (1965) *Manual of the Junior Personality Inventory*, London, University of London Press.

FINLAYSON, D.S. (1970) *Administrative Manual for School Climate Index, Administrative Manual for School Organisation Index*, Slough NFER.

FLEW, A. (1983) 'Schools on trial', *New Society*, 17 November, p. 290.

FLOUD, J. (1957) *Social Class and Educational Opportunity*, London, Heinemann.

FOGELMAN, K. (Ed.) (1983) *Growing Up in Great Britain*, London, Macmillan.

FOGELMAN, K. and HOLDEN, H. (1983) 'Examination results in selective and non-selective schools', *Concern*, summer, 48, pp. 6–9.

FOGELMAN, K. and RICHARDSON, K. (1974) 'School attendance: some results from the National Child Development Study', in TURNER, B. (Ed.) *Truancy*, London, Ward Lock.

FORD, J. (1969) *Social Class and the Comprehensive School*, London, Routledge and Kegan Paul.

FORD, J., MONGON, D. and WHELAN, M. (1983) *Special Education and Social Control: Invisible Disasters*, London, Routledge and Kegan Paul.

GAYLON, S. (1979) 'The Leicestershire story' in PLUCKROSE, H. and WILBY, P. (Eds) *The Condition of English Schooling*, Harmondsworth, Penguin.

GILBERT, J.P., LIGHT, R.J. and MOSTELLER, F. (1975) 'Assessing social innovations' in BENNETT, C.A. and LUMSDAINE, A.A. (Eds) *Evaluation and Experiment*, New York, Academic Press.

GILBERT, J.P. and MOSTELLER, F. (1972) 'The urgent need for experimentation' in MOSTELLER, F. and MOYNIHAN, F. (Eds) *On Equality of Education Opportunity*, New York, Random House.

GILLHAM, W.E.C. (Ed.) (1979) *Reconstructing Educational Psychology*, London, Croom Helm.

GILLHAM, W.E.C. (Ed.) (1981) *Problem Behaviour in the Secondary School*, London, Croom Helm.

GIPPS, C., STEADMAN, S., BLACKSTONE, T. and STIERER, B. (1983) *Testing Children*, London, Heinemann.

GITTINS, C. (Chairman) (1967) *Primary Education in Wales.* London, HMSO.

GRAY, J. and HANNON, V. (1986) 'HMI's interpretations of schools examination results', *Journal of Education Policy*, 1, 1.

GRAY, J., JESSON, D. and JONES, B. (1984) 'Prevailing differences in examination results between local education, authorities: Does school organization matter?', *Oxford Review of Education*, 10, 1, pp. 45–68.

GRAY, J., JESSON, D. and JONES, B. (1985) 'The verdict is still not proven', *Times Educational Supplement*, 26 July, p. 4.

GRAY, J., JESSON, D. and JONES, B. (1986) 'The search for a fairer way of comparing schools examination results', *Research Papers in Education*, 1, 2, pp. 92–122.

GRAY, J. and JONES, B. (1983) 'Disappearing data', *Times Educational Supplement*, 15 July, p. 4.

GRAY, J., MCPHERSON, A. and RAFFE, D. (1983) *Reconstructions of Secondary Education*, London, Routledge and Kegan Paul.

HALSEY, A.H. and GARDNER, L. (1953) 'Selection for secondary education and achievement in four grammar schools', *British Journal of Sociology*, March.

HAMMERSLEY, M. (1982) 'Ideology in the classroom: A critique of false consciousness', in BARTON, L. and WALKER, S. (Eds) *Schools, Teachers and Teaching*, Lewes, Falmer Press.

HAMMERSLEY, M. and WOODS, P. (1985) *Life in School: The Sociology of Pupil Culture*, Milton Keynes, Open University Press.

HARGREAVES, A. (1978) 'The significance of classroom coping strategies' in BARTON, L. and MEIGHAN, R. (Eds) *Sociological Interpretations of Schooling and Classrooms: A Reappraisal*, Driffield, Nafferton Books.

HARGREAVES, A. (1982) 'Contrastive rhetoric and extremist talk' in BARTON, L. and WALKER, S. (Eds) *Schools, Teachers and Teaching*, Lewes, Falmer Press.

HARGREAVES, D. (1981) 'Schooling for delinquency', in BARTON, L. and WALKER, S. (Eds) *Schools, Teachers and Teaching*, Lewes, Falmer Press.

HARGREAVES, D.H. (1967) *Social Relations in a Secondary School*, London, Routledge and Kegan Paul.

HARGREAVES, D.H. (1979) 'Durkheim, deviance and education' in BARTON, L. and MEIGHAN, R. (Eds) *Schools, Pupils and Deviance*, Driffield, Nafferton Books.

HARGREAVES, D.H. (1982) *The Challenge for the Comprehensive School*, London, Routledge and Kegan Paul.

HEATH, A. (1984) 'In defence of comprehensive schools', *Oxford Review of Education*, 10, 1, pp. 115–23.

HILSOM, S. and CANE, B. (1971) *The Teachers Day*, Slough, NFER

HIRSCHI, T. (1969) *Causes of Delinquency*, Berkeley, CA, University of California Press.

HOGGART, R. (1973) *Speaking to Each Other* (Vol. 1), Harmondsworth, Penguin.

HOLLY, D. (1963) *Social Class and Academic Selection in a London Comprehensive School*, unpublished MA thesis, University of London.

HOPKINS, A. (1979) *The School Debate*, Harmondsworth, Penguin.

HUNTER, C. (1983) 'Education and local government in the light of central government policy' in AHIER, J. and FLUDE, M. (Eds) *Contemporary Education Policy*, London, Croom Helm.

HUNTER, C. (1984) 'The political devaluation of comprehensives' in BALL, S.J. (Ed.) *Comprehensive Schooling: A Reader,* Lewes, Falmer Press.

JAMES, E. (1947) Article in *Times Educational Supplement*, 1 February.

JAMES, E. (1949) *The Content of Education*, London, Harrap.

JENKINS, R. (1959) *The Labour Case*, Harmondsworth, Penguin.

KENNEDY, M.F. (1981) 'The role of experiments in improving education' in ASLANIAN, C.B. (Ed.) *Improving Educational Evaluation Methods*, London, Sage.

KING, R. (1969) *School Organisation and Pupil Involvement*, London, Routledge and Kegan Paul.

KING, R. (1985) 'On the relative autonomy of education: micro/macro structures' in BARTON, L. and WALKER, S. (Eds) *Education and Social Change*, London, Croom Helm.

KINNOCK, N. (1986) 'New deal for our schools', *The Observer*, 30 March, p. 12.

KOSHE, G. (1957) *A Comparative Study of the Attainments and Intelligence of Children in Certain Comprehensive, Grammar and Secondary Modern Schools*, unpublished MA thesis, University of London.

LABOUR PARTY (1951) *A Policy for Secondary Education*, London, Labour Party.

LABOUR PARTY (1953) *Challenge to Britain*, London, Labour Party.

LABOUR PARTY (1958) *Learning to Live*, London, Labour Party.

LACEY, C. (1970) *Hightown Grammar*, Manchester, Manchester University Press.

LEFCOURT, H.M. (1976) *Locus of Control: Current Trends*, New York, John Wiley.

LOOSEMOORE, F.A. (1981) *Curriculum and Assessment in Wales — An Exploratory Study*, Cardiff, Schools Council for Wales.

LOWENSTEIN, L.F. (1979) 'How bright pupils slow down at comprehensives', *Weekly Educational Review*, 16 August, p. 2.

MADAUS, G.E., AIRASIAN, P.W. and KELLAGHAN, T. (1980) *School Effectiveness: A Re-assessment of the Evidence*, New York, McGraw Hill.

MARLAND, M. (1980) 'The pastoral curriculum' in BEST, R., JARVIS, C. and RIBBINS, P. (Eds) *Perspectives on Pastoral Care*, London, Heinemann.

MARSDEN, D. (1971) *Politicians Equality and Comprehensives*, (Fabian Tract 411), London, Fabian Society.

MAUDE, A. (1969) 'The egalitarian threat' in COX, C.B. and DYSON, A.E. (Eds) *Fight for Education: A Black Paper*, London, Critical Quarterly.

MAUGHAN, B. and RUTTER, M. (1987) 'Pupils progress in selective and non-selective schools', *School Organization*, 7.

MEASOR, L. and WOODS, P. (1984) *Changing Schools*, Milton Keynes, Open University Press.

MILES, H.B. (1979) *Some Factors Affecting Attainment at 18+*, London, Pergamon Press.

MILLER, T.W.G. (1961) *Values in the Comprehensive School*, London, Oliver and Boyd.

MINISTRY OF EDUCATION (1945) *The Nation's Schools*, London, HMSO.

MINISTRY OF EDUCATION (1947) *The New Secondary Education*, London, HMSO.

MONKS, T.G. (1968) *Comprehensive Education in England and Wales*, Slough NFER.

MONKS, T.G. (Ed) (1970) *Comprehensive Education in Action*, Slough, NFER.

MORGAN, C. (1980) 'The common core curriculum: Key issues for government', *Educational Research*, 22, 3, pp. 182–7.

MORTIMORE, P. (1986) *The Junior School Project: A Summary of the Main Report*, London, ILEA.

MORTON-WILLIAMS, R. and FINCH, S. (1968) *Enquiry 1*, London, HMSO.

MURGATROYD, S. and GRAY, H.L. (1982) 'Leadership and the effective school', *School Organization*, 2, pp. 285–96.

MURGATROYD, S.J. and REYNOLDS, D. (1984) 'Leadership and the teacher' in HARLING, P. (Ed.) *New Directions in Educational Leadership*. Lewes, Falmer Press.

MURGATROYD, S.J. and REYNOLDS, D. (1985) 'The creative consultant', *School Organization*, 4, 3, pp. 321–5.

MUSGROVE, F. and TAYLOR, H. (1969) *Society and the Teacher's Role*, London, Routledge and Kegan Paul.

NATIONAL UNION OF TEACHERS (Welsh Committee) (1975) *Qualifications for Entry into Sixth Forms in Secondary Schools in Wales*, Cardiff, NUT

NAYLOR, F. (1983) 'Proving worth in selective schools', *Times Educational Supplement*, 29 April, p. 4.

PARKINSON, M. (1970) *The Labour Party and the Organisation of Secondary Education 1918–1965*, London, Routledge and Kegan Paul.

PARTRIDGE, J. (1966) *Life in a Secondary Modern School*, Harmondsworth, Penguin.

PEARCE, J. (1986) *Standards and the LEA*, Slough, NFER/Nelson.

PEDLEY, R. (1969) *The Comprehensive School* (2nd Ed.), Harmondsworth, Penguin.

PHILLIPS, D. and DAVIE, R. (1985) 'Pathways for institutional development in secondary schools', in REYNOLDS, D. (Ed.) *Studying School Effectiveness*, Lewes, Falmer Press.

PRAIS, S.J. and WAGNER, K. (1985) 'Schooling standards in England and Germany: some summary comparisons bearing on economic performance', *National Institute Economic Review*, 112, May, pp. 53–76.

RADICE, G. (1986) 'Agenda for change', *Times Educational Supplement*, 9 May p. 4.

RAVEN, J.C. (1960) *Guide to the Standard Progressive Matrices*, London, H.K. Lewis.

REES, G.(1980) 'Educational inequality in Wales: some problems and paradoxes' in REES, G. and REES, T. (Eds) *Poverty and Social Inequality in Wales*, London, Croom Helm.

REID, M., CLUNIES-ROSS, L., GOACHER, B. and VILE, C. (1981) *Mixed Ability Teaching: Problems and Possibilities*. Slough NFER

REYNOLDS, D. (1975) 'When pupils and teachers refuse a truce' in MUNGHAM, G. and PEARSON, G. (Eds) *Working Class Youth Culture*, London, Routledge and Kegan Paul.

REYNOLDS, D. (1976) 'The delinquent school' in WOODS, P. (Ed.) *The Process of Schooling*, London, Routledge and Kegan Paul.

REYNOLDS, D. (1977) 'Towards a socio-psychological view of truancy' in DEPARTMENT OF HEALTH AND SOCIAL SECURITY *Working Together for Children and their Families*. London, HMSO

REYNOLDS, D. (1982a) 'The Welsh experience', *Secondary Education Journal*, 12, 3, pp. 24–6.

REYNOLDS, D. (1982b) 'The search for effective schools' *School Organization* 2, 3 pp. 215–37.

REYNOLDS, D. (1983) 'Welsh education: The problems and the promise', *Welsh Secondary Schools Review*, 70, 2, pp. 28–39.

REYNOLDS, D. (1984a) 'Relative autonomy reconstructed' *in* BARTON, L. and WALKER, S. (Eds) *Social Crisis and Educational Research*, London, Croom Helm.

REYNOLDS, D. (1984b) 'Creative conflict: The implications of recent educational research for those concerned with children', *Maladjustment and Therapeutic Education*, Spring, pp. 14–23.

REYNOLDS, D. (Ed.) (1985a) *Studying School Effectiveness*, Lewes, Falmer Press.

REYNOLDS, D. (1985b) 'The effective school', *Times Educational Supplement*, 20 September, p. 25.

REYNOLDS, D. (1986a) 'Managing the comprehensive school', *School Organization*, 6, 1, pp. 17–22.

REYNOLDS, D. (1986b) Discussion to paper by AITKEN, M. and LONGFORD, N. 'Statistical modelling issues in school effectiveness research', *Journal of the Royal Statistical Society* (Series A), 144, 1.

REYNOLDS, D. and JONES, D. (1978) 'Education and the prevention of juvenile delinquency' in TUTT, N.S. (Ed.) *Alternative Strategies for Coping with Crime*, Oxford, Basil Blackwell and Martin Robertson.

REYNOLDS, D., *et al.* (1987) *Bringing Schools Back In*. Lewes, Falmer Press.

REYNOLDS, D. and MURGATROYD, S.J. (1980) 'School factors and truancy' in HERSOV, L.A. and BERG, I. (Eds) *Out of School*, Chichester, John Wiley.

REYNOLDS, D. and MURGATROYD, S.J. (1981) 'Schooled for failure?', *Times Educational Supplement*, 4 December.

REYNOLDS, D. and MURGATROYD, S.J. (1983) 'Schooled for failure? (A restatement of the old evidence and an evaluation of the new evidence on the nature and causes of Welsh educational problems)', *Disaffection in Secondary Schools in Wales*, Cardiff, Schools Council for Wales.

REYNOLDS, D. and MURGATROYD, S.J. (1985) 'The greening of the valleys', *Times Educational Supplement*, 15 February, p. 22.

REYNOLDS, D. and MURGATROYD, S.J. (forthcoming) *A New Self-Concept Scale for Children*.

REYNOLDS, D. and REID, K. (1985) 'The second stage: Towards a reconceptualization of theory and methodology in school effectiveness research' in REYNOLDS, D. (Ed.) *Studying School Effectiveness*, Lewes, Falmer Press.

REYNOLDS, D. and SULLIVAN, M. (1979) 'Bringing schools back in' in BARTON, L. (Ed.) *Schools, Pupils and Deviance*, Driffield, Nafferton.

REYNOLDS, D. and SULLIVAN, M. (1980) 'Towards a new socialist sociology of education' in BARTON, L. (Ed.) *Schooling, Ideology and the Curriculum*, Lewes, Falmer Press.

REYNOLDS, D. and SULLIVAN, M. (1982) 'The comprehensive experience' in BARTON, L. and WALKER, S. (Ed.) *Schools, Teachers and Teaching*, Lewes, Falmer Press.

REYNOLDS, D. and SULLIVAN, M. (forthcoming) *The Transformative School*.

RISEBOROUGH, G.F. (1981) 'Teacher careers and comprehensive schooling: an empirical study', *Sociology*, 15, 3, pp. 355–81.

RODGERS, B. (1984) 'The trend of reading, standards re-assessed', *Educational Research*, 26, 3, pp. 153–66.

RUBENSTEIN, D. and SIMON, B. (1973) *The Evolution of the Comprehensive School 1926–1972*, London, Routledge and Kegan Paul.

RUTTER, M. *et al* (1979) *Fifteen Thousand Hours*, London, Open Books.

RUTTER, M. (1980) *Changing Youth in a Changing Society*, Oxford, Nuffield Provincial Hospitals Trust.

RUTTER, M. (1983) 'School effects on pupil progress — findings and policy implications', *Child Development*, 54, 1, pp. 1–29.

SARAN, R. (1973) *Policy Making in Secondary Education*, Oxford, Oxford University Press.

SAYER, J. (1985) *What Future for Secondary Schools?*, Lewes, Falmer Press.

SCHMUCK, R.R. (1978) 'Peer consultation for school improvement' in COOPER, C. and ALDERFER, C. (Eds) *Advances in Experiential Social Process*, London, Wiley.

SHAW, B. (1983) *Comprehensive Schooling: The Impossible Dream?* Oxford, Basil Blackwell.

SIKES, P.J., MEASOR, L. and WOODS, P. (1985) *Teacher Careers: Crises and Continuities*, Lewes, Falmer Press.

SIMON, B. (1974) *The Politics of Educational Reform 1920–1940*. London, Lawrence and Wishart.

SIMON, B. (1978) *Intelligence, Psychology and Education: A Marxist Critique*, London, Lawrence and Wishart.

SIMON, B. (1986) 'The battle of the blackboard', *Marxism Today*, June, pp. 20–6.

SMITH, D. (1979) 'Slow learners and the secondary school curriculum' in RUBENSTEIN, D. (Ed.) *Education and Equality*, Harmondsworth, Penguin.

SOCIETY OF TEACHERS OPPOSED TO PHYSICAL PUNISHMENT (STOPP) (1983) *One Every Nineteen Seconds*, London, STOPP

START, K.B and WELLS, B.K. (1972) *The Trend of Reading Standards*, Slough, NFER

STEEDMAN, J. (1980) *Progress in Secondary Schools*, London, National Children's Bureau.

STEEDMAN, J. (1983) *Examination Results in Selective and Non-Selective Schools*, London, National Children's Bureau.

STEVENS, A. (1980) *Clever Children in Comprehensive Schools*, Harmondsworth, Penguin.

SULLIVAN, M. (1987) *Sociology and Social Welfare*, London, George Allen and Unwin.

TIBBENHAM, A., ESSEN, J. and FOGELMAN, K. (1978) 'Ability grouping and school characteristics', *British Journal of Educational Studies*, 26, 1.

TOPPING, K. (1983) *Educational Systems for Disruptive Adolescents*, London, Croom Helm.

TURNER, C.H. (1969) 'An organisational analysis of a secondary modern school', *Sociological Review*, 17, 1 pp. 67–85.

TURNER, G. (1983) *The Social World of the Comprehensive School*, London, Croom Helm.

TYERMAN, M.J. (1968) *Truancy*, London, University of London Press.

VENNING, P. (1980) '"A" level absolutes', *Times Educational Supplement*, 18 January, p. 6.

VERNON, P.E. (Ed.) (1957) *Secondary School Selection*, London, Methuen.

VERNON, P.E. (1971) *Graded Arithemetic-Mathematics Test: Manual of Instructions*, London, University of London Press.

WALL, W.D. (1945) 'Reading backwardness among men in the army,' *British Journal of Educational Psychology*, 15, pp. 29–39.

WALSH, K., DUNNE, R., STEWART, J.D. and STOTEN, B. (1984) *Falling Rolls and the Management of the Teaching Profession*, Windsor, NFER.

WATTS, A.F. and VERNON, P.E. (1947) *Manual to the Watts-Vernon Reading Test*, London, Ministry of Education.

WEEKS, A. (1986) *Comprehensive Schools: Past, Present and Future*, London, Methuen.

WELSH EDUCATION OFFICE (1978) *Literacy and Numeracy, and Examination Achievements in Wales* (papers for the Mold Conference), Cardiff, Welsh Office.

WEST, D.J. (1982) *Delinquency*, London, Heinemann.

WILCOX, B. (1985) 'Conceptualizing curriculum differences for studies of secondary school effectiveness' in REYNOLDS, D. (Ed.) *Studying School Effectiveness*, Lewes, Falmer Press.

WILLMOTT, A.S. (1977) *CSE and 'O' Level Grading*, London, Macmillan.

WILSON, H. (1965) *The Relevance of Socialism*, London, Weidenfeld and Nicholson.

WOODS, P. (1979) *The Divided School*, London, Routledge and Kegan Paul.

WOODS, P. (1983) *Sociology and the School*, London, Routledge and Kegan Paul.

WRIGHT, N. (1977) *The Progress of Schooling*, London, Croom Helm.

YOUNG, M. (Ed.) (1971) *Knowledge and Control: New Directives for the Sociology of Education*, London, Collier-Macmillan.

Index